Awakening from the Midlife Chrysalis

Karen Wilson Pool

Learning Curves

Awakening
From the Midlife Chrysalis

Copyright © 2016,
Karen Wilson Pool

ISBN: 978-0-9672967-7-7

Published by Learning Curves, LLC
1055 North 1000 West,
Provo, UT 84604

Cover Design by Beth Jepson

Table of Contents

Introduction   5

Chapter 1 – The Call   11

Chapter 2 – The Doorway   25

Chapter 3 – First Steps   37

Chapter 4 – The Long Hallway   51

Chapter 5 - Descent   73

Chapter 6 – The Room in the Middle   95

Chapter 7 – Shedding   117

Chapter 8 – Emergence   131

Chapter 9 – Congruence   147

Resources & Recommended Reading   165

Acknowledgements   169

Introduction

Midlife is a hot topic these days, especially since baby boomers—76 million strong—began sprinting through the 50s into what Angeles Arrien calls the wisdom years, ages 60-100. Not so in 1900 when the average life span was 48 years. Many never saw their children raised, played with grandchildren, or retired from everyday work to a life of leisure or volunteer contribution. The infant mortality rate was high because of diseases that have been virtually eliminated through the use of vaccines. In addition, mothers today rarely die in childbirth. By 1967, the average life span increased to 68. Today it's approximately 80-84. Because of medical advances, many of us survive heart attacks, cancer, and life-threatening accidents.

Over the past century, the midlife goal line has moved. Many baby boomers plan to work into their 70s, not pausing for a moment. Our extended life span offers us a vantage point at midlife unheard of in earlier generations. This is a time in our lives when we may feel an urge to enter the interior landscape of our heart because the answers from outside of us may cease to satisfy our desires for meaning and contribution.

The term midlife crisis often doesn't fit, mental health experts say, because while it can be accompanied by serious depression, it can also mark a period of tremendous growth. It's really another time of transition—between one age of our lives gone and the new one not yet established. We sense that we are called to do something new, yet there are no well-worn paths or experienced people to show us the way. Our curiosity and desire to contribute or participate in forming our future push us into the unknown. We are seeking our unique melody that will enable us to sing with courage from our authentic center. This is essential to our being and becoming. What insights will our generation leave for the next ones, to prepare them for developmental stages that may include a period of inner work at midlife?

Erik Erikson, the first psychologist to view the life cycle by stages, referred to life unfolding in observable sequence, "each stage marked by a turning point, a crucial period of increased vulnerability and heightened potential." Gail Sheehy suggests that these transitional or developmental stages are "defined by changes that begin *within*."

The sages and wisdom leaders of the ages have championed this contemplative life. For instance, in the *Hero's Journey*, Joseph Campbell suggests that just before the hero reaches the Supreme Ordeal, he or she will come to a point he refers to as "The Belly of the Whale," a reference to Jonah entering the whale in the biblical story. By entering this stage, the person shows a willingness to undergo a metamorphosis, to die to him or herself. "This popular motif gives emphasis to the lesson that the crossing of the threshold resembles an adventure from which there is no going back. But instead of passing outward the hero goes inward, to be born again."

As with most earth-linked processes, I've wondered if this interior journey has its own cycle—stages and signposts that let us know where we stand in any particular moment. This time of reflection for me began with the image of a caterpillar unraveling in a chrysalis. When I tore apart my first draft of this book last year to start over again—a moment of trust—immediately the ideas for new chapter titles came into my mind. I captured them quickly. It was as if I stood at the entrance to an interior metaphorical structure. Writing this book provided a way for me to order and share the perplexities, insights, and discoveries of my own journey. Each chapter encourages an awakening to where I am and perhaps you are—to face the fears that keep us from moving forward into authentic living for the rest of our days.

Chapter 1
The Call

*"We all have islands of fear inside us,
and we also have continents of wisdom and
truth. How do we find our way to them when
we are not educated in the interior dimension?
These inner landscapes hold the patterns of our
passions and purpose. Without knowing how to
journey there, our lives remain unlived."*
—Dawna Markova

Several years ago, somewhere within
the recesses of my being, I heard a compelling
call into stillness and reflection, which I stead-
fastly ignored. Our four children were grown
and moving toward independent living. My
husband had recently invested our retirement
in a new business venture. I was working in a
fulltime administrative position that provided
financial support and much-needed medical

insurance, an ongoing reservoir of valuable friendships, and blessed oblivion into workaholism. I received a great deal of pleasure from working hard and being productive without any thought of possible long-term consequences.

A typical day started with an early rise to exercise, and bracketed time for meetings with department heads and student organization officers. Then I rushed to another building to teach a university course. This particular semester I was also auditing a Spanish class across campus. There was no time for lunch on these teaching days, and I wore a pedometer to count the 10,000 to16,000 steps I took daily as part of the university's "get healthy" plan. I came home to prepare a quick supper and pushed through the exhaustion to a second wind. Then I prepped for the next class in two days, watched a TV show with my husband, worked on a grant until 11 p.m. and toppled over into bed. "Stillness," I thought. "Sounds ridiculous! I don't have time to be Henry David Thoreau."

Those of us who wear ourselves out with our busy lives would be envious of Thoreau and the time he took for reflection and thought. Although many assume that he led his simple life in isolation, he often visited the town of Concord, was a regular at the table of Emerson, and invited others to his cabin for discussions. Unremarkable to historians, his mother, Cynthia, and sisters Helen and Sophia, cleaned, washed, and mended his clothes and brought meals in during the two years he spent at Walden Pond.

In stark contrast to Thoreau, my thinking time usually came in micro snatches and had little depth of insight or connecting arrangement. Instead, those random thoughts

most often resulted in extensive to-do lists
that I would add to off and on throughout
the day, filling in the week ahead to the brim.
Even God didn't get a word in edgewise and
waited until 4 a.m. when I was still and slight-
ly rested, to share the insights and answers I
sought.

A call to stillness was as foreign to me
as walking on water and seemingly just as
impossible.

The thought has crossed my mind that
in addition to the addiction I have to doing too
much, I also have a tendency to connect stillness with laziness or inefficiency.

My encouragement to work began as a
young child and I've carried the attitude and
discipline of beginning and finishing what I
start and the work required to do so, into every aspect of my adult life.

I review this dilemma of un-training

these engrained and hardened habits, feeling
the pressure to produce, the high of filling
every moment, and how easily I skirt around
being still, like a skittish and nervous pony
avoiding a bear in a mountain path. Why
this urgent call to stillness? Why this feeling
that I need to undo habits that have served
me so well so far, and what will I do with my
never-ending list of things I could do? On the
other hand, what harm will it do to slow down
for a while and create a different rhythm and
space around the things I love to do?

Once in a while I proudly tape these to-
do lists into my journal to remind myself that
yes, like my pioneer ancestors, and in spite of
labor saving devices and other conveniences
available to my generation, I can also work
from dawn to dusk. I'm not mending clothes
by candlelight, but I'm up as late as I can be
finishing up one project or another. I'm in a

hardwired rhythm. It doesn't seem to be a good time to make major changes.

As I look back, the first assumption I made in my twenties was false. I thought that when I became an adult, I would be the same person for the rest of my life—fully formed. I would always know what to do, or someone would counsel me and I would move forward easily. That is just not the case. This surprised me, and perhaps others, who like me, expected life to transition smoothly through marriage and children to the empty nest and into some sort of contribution later in life. I did not anticipate or chart the interior changes, the refiner's fire experiences, or the smoldering, underground forces that shaped my life as well. Loss, disappointment, and trauma were not experiences I plotted onto my life's goal sheet.

Now fast forward ten years to the mid

1980s. I was in my mid-thirties and restless. Ten years of marriage and we were no more settled than when my husband and I began life together. We were nomads—a few years in Mississippi, then several more in my husband's hometown in Texas before we landed in the West. The first crisis was a financial one. We spent five months apart, waiting for our Mississippi home to sell. Twelve months later, to avoid making two house payments, we gave that home away. We had four little children ages five and under. I had my bachelor's degree and no marketable skills. I spent every spare moment working odd jobs and trying to figure out how to respond and not just react to the anxiety I felt on a daily basis. I hadn't developed the capacity for much of an internal dialogue.

In fact, I knew very little about my own thinking. I only knew that I shut down

when I was frustrated or worried or angry.
As a result, I would stay anxious for hours,
ruminating on what wasn't working, like an
airplane hovering in the sky with no place to
land. When I did this, my perspective dimin-
ished, and all I could see were roadblocks and
limits. I knew how to work hard and complete
any task where step-by-step instruction was
available, but was clueless if what I needed
to do wasn't laid out for me or required my
own innovation. I had developed no tools with
which to forge a new direction, and so I had to
invent a new way of thinking and responding.

Over time I began an internal process
of inquiry. As I was attentive, I learned that
each time fear or anxiety filled my heart, I
would arrive at a point of choice, and it was
inside of myself that the transformation would
take place. I suppose I stood in the middle of
one of those turning points—fully alive, seek-

ing solutions, and some measure of security in the face of uncertainty. I determined to open myself and learn. I became sensitized to the depletion of energy that comes from worry, anxiety, anger, and despair.

My frustration became curiosity and served as a catalyst for action, although initially I didn't know what direction to take. Despite this inner tinkering with my thinking patterns, I wanted to go into hiding or have someone else fix everything so I didn't have to work so hard. In the midst of uncertainty, I moved forward because standing still didn't give me any measure of peace. No fairy godmother appeared on the scene to rescue me. I took a couple of courses at the junior college and worked part-time when I could.

Our move to the Rocky Mountains brought me close to a university. My growth centered in student teaching and graduate school. Our four young children attended elementary school, and my husband was in the early stages of launching a new company with a former boss. Our home in Texas stayed on the market for three years before we finally sold it at a loss. As I taught at a high school during the day and to adults at night, I realized I preferred working with adult learners. I came to the end of student teaching and felt clueless about how to pursue a career in education without having to teach high school full time.

This became both an earthshaking and beneficial transition that launched an unexpected career path as an instructional writer and educational trainer assigned to work with junior and high school educators from more than a dozen school districts. It was also the first time I experimented with thinking outside the box and trusting the answers that came from within.

• • •

Now, two decades later, I find I have
tumbled forward into another inner, tumul-
tuous, and undefined space that refuses to
fit into my well-thought-out 5-year plan. As
I've grown older, I've learned that adulthood
contains more dimension and depth—more
peaks and valleys—than one lengthy, smooth
plateau leading downward toward old age
and death. Even so, I find myself still expect-
ing that comfortable landing place where one
coasts for a while. Instead, my life constantly
tilts one way or another, forcing minor adjustments. Children, financial ups and downs,
and health issues stretch me beyond the
bounds of my comfort zone—and again, more
questions arise than answers.

In the swirl and blur that comes with
speed and productivity, an essential part of

me suffocates. Not the creative part. There is plenty of that. Some other part continues to be covered over with a mat of overgrown vines that need to be torn through like the unwieldy creeping grape and overgrown weigela bushes in my backyard that I dug out last fall.

Here I sit in the North House at Aldermarsh on Whidbey Island, Washington. I've come to a writing workshop that offers learning and space in a lush, peaceful setting. I wanted to create an opening—a stake in the ground of my busy life—to tell the truth: the overindulgent life I've lived must die and make room for one that is more mindful, simple, and less rushed.

It's the fourth day of the workshop and Christina, our facilitator, has us choose a writing card from a box without looking. Mine says, "SLOW DOWN." I smile and shake my head. Even here the universe has found a way to send a message. Initially I ask, "How does the hummingbird in my heart, even an exhausted one, slow down?" This is where transformation comes in. I can choose another metaphor for my life, something more se-rene—a swan at rest in an evening setting, for instance. Or one that offers some breathing space and down time without feeling pressure to check something off a list. Could I live with-out a list? I'm not sure . . .

Perhaps some people do not encounter this particular developmental stage at mid-life—an urge for time apart inside the silent chrysalis facing an unknown inner journey. I'm honestly, although reluctantly acknowl-edging an important transition I have ne-glected earlier. The trick, I suppose, comes in inventing a schedule and space for contempla-tion—designing and extending the boundaries of stillness that will work for *me*, not necessarily for Thoreau or some other male who has "behind the scenes" support. I have learned that life fills up with what seems most expedient "to do," not what is most expedient "to not do." And so I'm brought to the following anonymous quote, and if resonates with you also, read further.

What in your life
is calling you?

When all the noise is silenced,
the meetings adjourned,
the lists laid aside,
and the wild iris blooms
by itself in the dark forest,
what still pulls on your soul?

In the silence between your
heartbeats hides
a summons.

Do you hear it?

Chapter 2
The Doorway

"For all the years we spend in formal education, we receive virtually no instruction about our inner life. Eventually, there comes a turning point when attention shift to what is going on in one's inner world—how to purposefully shape our thoughts and behaviors to optimize our ability to reach our goals."
—Linda Austin

I stand at the threshold, aware of a process that has been awaiting my attention for some time. It surfaces again and again—this urge to stop everything I feel essential and desirable. Only a small part of me, though, wants to sit in a shady spot in the garden and document the inner journey. I struggle to illuminate the deeper yearnings tugging at my heart. These surround my life's purpose, ultimately determining how I will spend the rest of my days. The image of a chrysalis continually comes to mind. I feel somewhat dismantled in the process, not unlike the caterpillar unraveling in a chrysalis, and give in to anxiety, alternating with curiosity. Just as a caterpillar undergoes transformation, the initial structures of my life struggle to be broken down so that new ones can form.

Richard Bode tells of his experience with stillness when he had to wear a plaster cast from chest to toes for six months following hip surgery:

> "Day after day, as I lay in my enforced idleness, I thought deeply about who I was, where I came from, and what I wanted to be. There is a secret to stillness. From this place of calm arises an awareness that is far more acute

than when we're plunging mindlessly through life. What we lose in motion we gain in insight, which is a movement of another kind."

This encourages me and I ponder what I will change. I'm not in a plaster cast. I'm in an immobilizing cast of my own choosing that I want to break apart. This bone-deep exhaustion I feel has come from doing many good things and has been part of my life for so long it's difficult to imagine anything different. How does one choose stillness when grandchildren race through the door, and it's most comfortable to extend past roles indefinitely? I easily numb myself against interior's uncertain song. I hear only a small echo drumming its consistent beat in the shadow of my heart: "You must grow again in a distinctly different way, apart from all you know."

The few steps ahead in my life's

journey—including this path inward— show
nothing clearly. I sense only that confusion
and chaos accompany this step over the
threshold into the unknown. In fact, options
sit like a stack of closed books. Which ones
will I open? I intuitively realize, and this is
where the resistance comes, that what I've
learned and experienced previously that has
broken me open will not carry me forward
or keep me from stumbling through the next
murky and uncertain phase. I will be forging
through new ground to find the light and insight I seek. Angeles Arrien explains,

> "A threshold suggests the place or
> moment where transformational work,
> learning, or integration occurs. Figu-
> ratively, the threshing floor is where
> we tread, turn, twist, or flail as we do
> inner work. Instinctively, we recognize
> that we are required to let go of what

is familiar and open ourselves to the unknown."

I choose to step into this unknown, uneasy searching of the depths of my heart, thoughts, and feelings, alternatively satisfied and frustrated that my specific molting process will not be generated from the advice and experience of others. It will be developed within the cauldron of impressions I receive from my inner guide.

This process requires surrender, rather than control, trusting the integrity of my own inner process. It feels like a nowhere between endings and beginnings. It's a place of disorder—one day hopeful, the next hopeless; two days forward, then one day backward. Nothing makes sense. I must keep going, even though at times I'm overwhelmed. Clarity comes and goes. Finally I stumble into the way through: I embrace the uncertainty. I let go of the when's and how's. I stop creating lengthy to-do lists of distracting and productive assignments that I will slide in on the side when I'm still.

I turn toward my heart, which yearns for stillness—to write and paint and eventually study Spanish again. I let the space of quiet and contemplation stretch out some days. I putter and rest and take small steps forward. Trusting myself helps me sustain the tension of not knowing what's ahead. There are moments when it's surprisingly enjoyable—this space between beginnings and endings. Still, I'm anxious . . .

I search for a handhold in a boat tossed about on the waves and into the entrance of a new uncertain and undefined turning point. My best clue that I'm seeking the quick fix without the required threshing work comes when I realize I'm mooching someone else's idea about what worked for them. Their usual responses include encouraging and well-founded advice about the direction and substance of what needs to happen. When I imagine what my life would be like according to what they offer, it's as if I'm fitting myself into an over-sized or too-tight sweater. Either I can't breathe or I trip over the hem.

On the other hand, if I pause when I feel restless and itchy, as though I am shedding some inner, invisible skin, I remember that periodic seasons of reassessment provide time for necessary introspection. I chip away at the "cast of exhaustion" by becoming more aware of my needs for rest and creative space, prioritizing my inner strivings instead of being at the beck and call of everyone else first. I know this is important; otherwise I will continually make a false start.

In racing, a "false start" occurs when a sprinter sets off from the blocks too early.

When this occurs, the runners have to stop, return to the blocks, and start over again. Unless I clear any negative or tired-worn habitual internal messages, I'll bump into psychological and emotional demands—an unrelenting stream of expectations that will push me into a wall of anxiety partway through and into a stall. I won't be ready. The false start illuminates an external manifestation of internal messages, a set of unidentified (minimized or denied) "have to's" and "ought to's." Preventing a false start begins with an exploration that builds stronger internal boundaries and strengthens integrity and character.

I want to become patient through the stall and interior squall, trusting that even in the smallest breach in my gut's weather pattern, I will hear the whisper that brings clarity. Choosing this nudge toward inner growth, I decide to accept the emotional ups and downs and internal shifting winds that bend me to my knees. I must become sensitive to new patterns of meaning and perspective that may surface.

Outwardly I appear distracted and could be accused of not paying attention to details I usually manage. Much of the time I do caretaking on autopilot. I will gradually develop a plan to disengage from my university job and the intensity of our ongoing and consuming social calendar of obligation and connection. Then part of me wonders what to do when I'm all by myself.

I'm not going into hibernation like a bear, sleeping winter away in a mountain cave. I need some time out. Not the kind of time out that has become a common parenting technique. Most of us don't think to use it ourselves when we become crusty, like a boat that needs to be raised up so the barnacles can be scraped away. Even when life on the surface continues at an unrelenting pace, as it does for many, I will watch for moments when I can enter the depth of my being and sit, patiently at ease with introspective questions, such as these:

- What brings me to life?
- What's worth doing with the balance of my time on earth?
- What untapped gifts or talents do I wish to explore?
- Have I expressed my life and values in a sufficiently beautiful way?
- Who am I when I stop doing—when I'm not the caretaker or educator/ administrator, etc. any more?
- What is unfinished for me to learn, to experience?

• Am I leaving a legacy that enables others to live better?

I have asked similar questions in earlier stages of life, yet they return again, differently phrased, and with offspring of their own, looking for deep and fertile ground in which to seed themselves.

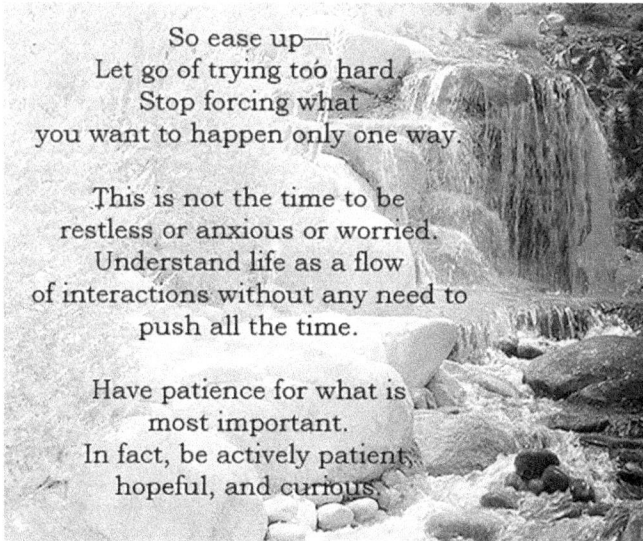

So ease up—
Let go of trying too hard.
Stop forcing what
you want to happen only one way.

This is not the time to be
restless or anxious or worried.
Understand life as a flow
of interactions without any need to
push all the time.

Have patience for what is
most important.
In fact, be actively patient,
hopeful, and curious.

Chapter 3
First Steps

"It is essential to claim the pause and find in this new search the aliveness and meaning that will make the years ahead more precious."
—Gail Sheehy

My first steps felt unsure, unsteady, and unpredictable, since what I move toward seemed unclear. I haven't ever finished one aspect or transition in my life without knowing clearly what would come next. The significant message was to wait—wait for what? Just wait . . . and breathe. It's difficult enough to wait in a busy doctor's office or in line at a grocery store at 5 p.m. Waiting just to wait feels unsettling. As Sue Monk Kidd tells it, "[I must] practice the ability to dwell in unknowing, to live inside a question, and coexist with the tensions of uncertainty." I decided to honor the nudge urging me to clear a landing strip in the forest of over activity in my life—an entry-way for my spirit to settle. It didn't happen all at once.

Even when I left full-time administrative work at the university, I kept teaching an online course I had developed a decade earlier. Then without a pause I offered to pilot a new online course. Two weeks before the new semester began, I only had the first lesson materials and assignments from someone else who was developing the course. Before I knew it, sixty students enrolled. The new course was so poorly written that it became its own part-time job. I critiqued the course in frantic detail each week and emailed responses to an overload of student assignments and discussion board questions.

The next semester, distance education admitted the cap for the course should have been 45 students. I found that many of the course problems I identified hadn't been fixed. I also discovered the modify button, deleted irrelevant assignments and those that required students to provide personal information to Internet sites to retrieve data, and revised what wasn't fixed yet. This, besides frequent travel, sometimes helping my mother-in-law in Texas, creative life planning presentations where I could sell my books, and blessed time with grandchildren, kept my schedule full of structure, assignments, and meaningful obligations.

I've been unraveling my life ever since, distinguishing those activities and projects that bring happiness and contentment. The first milestone toward a more introspective life came when I let go of teaching the pilot course; someone else could wrestle with that debacle. Two years later I turned the other online course over to a qualified colleague and freed myself from university life.

I found that time off, time out, time for quiet reflection does not happen as an accepted part of our societal responsibilities. While I was teasing apart the many strands of my daily existence, I stayed antsy and willingly took on any neighborly or community assignment that came my way. Unable to resist another creative project, I picked up the thread of a coming-of-age fiction story and began writing a draft of a chapter every two weeks.

Time for silence and reflection still eludes me, although I now avoid pushing through in the evening, seeking a second wind. That is the next milestone. Now I stop sometime in the late afternoon and relax most evenings. I'm slowly learning that overextending myself and still covering too many bases is not stretching myself in the way my soul is craving.

During the past few years, even though some of my friends and family don't believe me, I've been rethinking the importance of mindful living that includes quiet space. I must create time for reflection and play in order to rediscover hidden and joyous parts of myself in a way that is healthy. Life can be simplified. There are times when I work and write. Some days I let myself relax into a slower rhythm with no agenda or to-do list. I'm not encumbered with fixing meals or paying bills or running errands. I read whatever I want, rather than what I feel is required for research. I practice letting go of schedules and time—where efficiency rules and productivity is the end result.

For decades I've created to-do lists minus the balancing alternatives of playtime or downtime of any kind. Changing all of this requires thought and less busyness. I did stop living unconsciously. I started looking at all the projects, activities, and goals, and decided I would figure out what I could cross off or set aside.

As I search for clarity, my heart serves as a measuring stick rather than the pursuit of money, obligations, prestige, or accolades. When I still my busy mind and create a space for what my heart desires, even it if takes time, I can trust that the answer will come. In the meantime, I listen. I've become content with the silent spaces of the inner journey, which is encouraging. It means I have released the *monkey mind* that chatters worry, stress, frustration, and fear. When these disturbing thoughts appear, I've learned to acknowledge them and express gratitude, as that emotion has the highest electromagnetic vibration and helps me move into a place of curiosity.

Journaling has become an important tool that can assist this process—a place to capture my search for questions, and responses to untangle myself from to everyday dilemmas. Stefali Tsabary suggests, "Write without thinking about what you're going to put on paper. Simply record your stream of consciousness. Such writing loosens the ego hold and you dip into the stillness that lies beneath, where your true self resides."

I want to examine some of the dreams that I have placed on the back burner for years, as well as new ones. The self I have developed and adapted to the people and circumstances that surround me has to change. And it's not as though I'm dropping breadcrumbs so that

I can return to a place I've left behind. Rather, it's more like casting a fishing line forward and then holding on to the line as I move through the darkness, trusting that I'll gradually come into the light. Clarity may come as the slow melt of a glacier, rather than in an instant as I would wish.

These stages of inner transformation manifest themselves in irregular and highly individualized ways. I'm unsure, for some reason now, which causes me to stall in my process. Some kind of inner confusion or imbalance stays with me. Perhaps it's because no one stands ahead in the distance, beckoning me or showing the way. I meander back and forth in my thinking as if searching for a way through an unfamiliar mountain pass. I come to a clearing and see the vista—a possible destination and confidently move forward only to lose it again in the underbrush. I'm reminded often these days that any transformational process entails taking things at a slower pace and going deeper into the creative and intuitive process. I will feel my way through.

When this feeling of confusion persists, whether the exterior of my life is stable or uncertain, everything else in my world must usually continue on. Nothing outwardly changes, and I recognized this type of underground stirring earlier in my life, prompting me to look inward.

Two patterns have emerged in my life previously. One is where I took initiative and invented my life through a series of experimental actions—how I ended up in an unconventional graduate program, for instance. The other came because of outside forces that prompted a response—my husband changing jobs where we experienced lengthy financial downturns several times over the years. In either case, I increased in resiliency and growth and self-trust. To not be "busy doing" all the time requires me to trust my inner metronome to a more relaxed tempo.

Gail Sheehy cautions, "If one cannot dare the broadening that is a universal urge [at this time], or pretends the crises of development don't exist, not only will they rise up later, but hit with a greater wallop. In the meantime we don't grow." The pathway through this interior passage and the deep questions I encounter, I trust, will lead me ultimately into a fuller development of an authentic and alive self, although it's difficult to realize this in the moment. This call to stillness and reflection cannot be forced; it must be answered willingly.

At this juncture, I face the discomfort with brutal honesty, trusting I will find my way eventually to a place where more of my

true self shines through. My unknowingness
may cause me to stumble, and it's easiest to
keep the radio of life's volume raised on the
complexities of my exterior life, drowning out
the soft, encouraging voice drawing me inward
toward an unexpected place of calm, clarity,
and peace.

Initially, this documentation process pro-
duces random and disconnected thoughts—no
revealing patterns, nothing that makes sense.
Continued effort will yield gems of insight. I've
kept a record of much of my life in the form of
events. This serves as a preliminary practice
as the patterns of the inner journey arise in
images and metaphors requiring interpreta-
tion.

Janet Conner writes, "Deep soul writing
is about asking questions until you uncover
the ones you've never asked. Its purpose is to
deliver the guidance you need right now to live

the full, rich life you are here to live."

These questions from James Hollis support reflection:

> • What has brought me to this point in my life?
>
> • How have I chosen this life I lead, these consequences?
>
> • What forces shaped me, perhaps diverted me, or wounded me?
>
> • What other forces supported me and are still at work within me?
>
> • What characteristics and talents will I bring forward into my newly formed life?

As I searched for a description of where I stand at this stage of my own journey, it feels as though I am riding along in an upside down car—seat-belted in, though surprisingly without any concern of falling out. The image disturbed me until I wrote about it, realizing that I was still safe in the journey, and that I could relish the new perspective the ride offered. This image of safety amid uncertainty is a recurring theme.

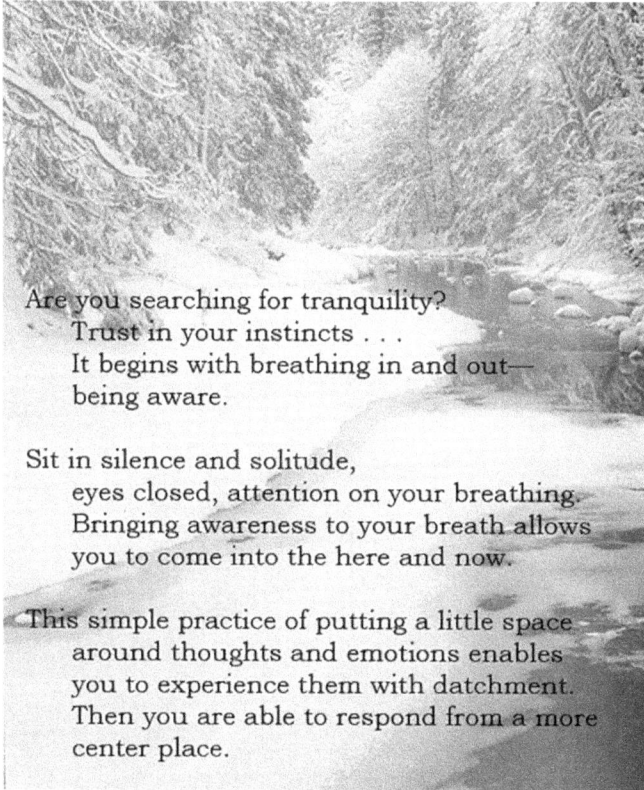

Are you searching for tranquility?
    Trust in your instincts . . .
    It begins with breathing in and out—
    being aware.

Sit in silence and solitude,
    eyes closed, attention on your breathing.
    Bringing awareness to your breath allows
    you to come into the here and now.

This simple practice of putting a little space
    around thoughts and emotions enables
    you to experience them with datchment.
    Then you are able to respond from a more
    center place.

Chapter 4
The Long Hallway

"At some point, usually later in life, we begin at last to let the soul lead. And though the soul does not assume the lead by killing off the ego, the ego is demoted and given a different assignment in the psyche, which is essentially to submit to the concerns of the soul."
—Clarissa Pinkola Estes

Time and time again, I've settled into the review that seems to be the next step, only to be distracted by something else I think needs to be done. The doer and go-all-the-time part of me enjoys having ten things I can turn to that distract me—stuffing my schedule like a room from the Victorian age: overfilled to the point of clutter. The caretaker in me absorbs others' needs quickly and effortlessly as well. Now that I'm slowly, slowly un-encumbering and ready, I find some sort of assessment surfacing.

A shadow of light appears as I take a step into what looks like a dim hallway. With the light comes insight: It's my long hallway. Snatches of images and impressions emerge as if I'm watching a scattering of movie sound bites. There are some pictures on the walls and others on the floor. These reveal masks I've worn to partially or fully hide my true identity, roles I may have over-identified with, unhealthy traditions of my family and culture, and other habits or attitudes or shadows that must be dismantled before new life can take hold. In addition, I've found myself addicted, not only to productivity, but also to stress, worry, a need for control, and a tendency to numb or stuff emotions.

These images illustrate where my authentic self has been realized and others that show some remnant of shadow side. "Our shadow side," teaches Robert Masters, "contains the emotions and desires we've disowned, neglected, or hidden from ourselves." I'm shedding light on what has been unconscious. Carl Jung states: "Our shadow is all that we think we are not, and emerges in an attempt to bring greater balance into our lives."

I have been happy in the roles I've chosen as well as the talents I've developed through my university career. I'm proud of my family heritage that encourages study and hard work. Our roles define us to a degree, and when they change, there is a letting go process. This reminds me of what occurs inside the chrysalis where the caterpillar digests itself, releasing enzymes to dissolve all of its tissues. I am willing to examine old perception and habits that get in my way.

I take a deep breath and move deeper into the hallway. This is not a critique, rather "seeing"—looking at the accumulation of roles, attitudes, and habits, and seeking an inner wisdom, the learning, and what needs to remain going forward. What parts of all I have become still carry shadows? What parts of these identities require softening and release and which are the authentic pieces of me that I will treasure past midlife?

A collage of images—sixty years' worth of experiences—moves slowly through my mind. I consider all that has made me who I am, as if I'm looking into a mirror or reflection: the helper, the expectation as the oldest child to be the perfect example, the pleaser, the achiever, the anxious budgeter, the workaholic, the educator, the curious learner, the music lover, the light seeker, the instructional writer, wife, mother, God's friend, the worrier, the questioner, the creator, the controller, the warrior, the scarcity thinker. Four images rise to the surface encouraging me to explore further in depth to see what I learn from looking at the shadow side.

The first image is **The Caretaker**. In adulthood the socially acceptable female caretaker does it all as wife, mother, and community or school volunteer with silent contentment, and sometimes surrenders herself in the process. The most important characteristics are duty and sacrifice, not creativity or joy or even wholeness.

As the oldest daughter, I learned this early when my curious nature got me in trouble and spanked often. I'm sure I exasperated my mother who didn't need me to continually get into drawers and cupboards. By the time

I was five, four additional children had been born and she taught me to fold clothes and diapers, stir Jello or gravy, peel potatoes, and play with and feed my baby sister.

Reading was important and my mother often read to us. Eventually I preferred reading alone in my bedroom or out in my hammock made of used baling twine in the chokecherry trees south of our home until called for the next assignment to help. I savored my alone time, and didn't realize how much the introverted part of me needed to recover energy after spending any amount of time with others. I became chief assistant cook, house cleaner, gardener, laundress (it seemed we were always hanging out clothes, diapers, sheets, and towels), and babysitter of small children. I began piano lessons at age seven, and piano practice added to my assignments. Around age thirteen, I became the organist in our church worship service when my piano teacher, the organist in my small community, moved away.

That same summer I learned to sew in 4-H (now there were eight children) and became the seamstress of a number of dresses for myself and my three, and eventually four other sisters—shifts with sleeves, zippers, and Peter Pan collars or jumpers in a variety of cotton solids and prints. I even sewed clothes for my sisters' dolls. Even though the initial efforts were gosh-awful, my ability improved with practice.

I kept sewing for years to help out and save money, including a year of custom projects. One day I realized that I didn't really enjoy sewing clothing all that much and most often could buy items on sale for much less than the cost of fabric and my time. Now I piece quilts—a leisurely color play activity I enjoy that doesn't require gathers, collars with piping or lace edging, set-in sleeves, French seams, buttonholes, or zippers. Everything I learned then became a service that I gave willingly to my family and community. Caretaking has continued throughout my life.

The shadow side of helping is resentment—outwardly nice; inwardly seething, and perhaps even unconscious of what's happening inside initially. When I'm always on call without any relief or time out for self-care, I dry out and become stiff with anger, like an over-starched shirt. Even though I now include myself in the family circle of needs and wants, I check my body for any residual feelings of resentment—any repressed or denied part of myself. I could do better about clarifying the boundary around my need for quiet, creativity, and writing space. I could express my desires and timelines for their fulfillment.

Instead of suppressing my feelings of frustration when I'm past my sell-by date for the
day or week, I've learned the fine art of saying
"No," or, "Maybe another time," and "Perhaps
you could do that yourself, or "Check with me
later. I'm taking a much-deserved nap."

The Pleaser shows up next. Pleasing
others is another stereotypical expectation of
women, and we're sometimes taught to disre-
gard our own wishes. Part of pleasing others is
appropriate—to help out, maintain harmony,
and show sensitivity to others' needs. When
personal desires are ignored or dismissed
without discussion or opportunity, the message comes through clearly: "When opinions
and desires don't match what "we" think is
important, keep them to yourself." Or, without
knowing, we put our own pleasures and ourselves last, stuffed away in a forgotten corner
of resignation and disappointment. In the

process I sacrificed some dreams, and never discovered my "self" or my voice until years later.

Even though I've resolved my feelings about a particular incident, it still stands out as an example of this in my own life. From the time I was very young, my parents played recordings of classical music and I learned the names of various instruments. Even though I took piano lessons, I dreamed of playing the violin. In our small community, at age 13 we're old enough to attend the three-week summer music school where soon-to-be junior high students could choose an instrument.

When the music teacher asked me about my choice, I said, "I want to play the violin." I didn't know the music summer school was band only.

"No." he said, "You want to play the clarinet."

My parents agreed. So without any protest,
I learned to play the clarinet, and played in
band and orchestra through high school, and
even a year in college.

The shadow side of pleasing is self-
denial and practiced unfamiliarity with what
one wants. I can remember many things I was
told to do or think that pleased others. I can
still feel the underpinnings of early expectations. When I give into these without reviewing
them in context with what pleases me, they
erode my sense of self. Through some refining
experiences during my middle thirties I really
began to think for myself and decide what I
wanted in life without feeling guilty.

My parents were both fine educators, so
it seemed natural for me to become a teacher.
Even though I initially became certified as a
high school teacher, my best work occurred
at the university level with adult learners. I

worked and taught at the university for many years and found it stimulating and rewarding. Deep inside though, I yearned to be a writer, and yet I couldn't conceive of writing as a vocation outside of teaching until I studied instructional writing in graduate school. During my university years, I wrote curriculum and instructional materials on the side. Book ideas percolated and stayed locked in my heart. I've been inspired by Madeleine L'Engle's story:

> After roughly 40 rejection letters, her agent gave up and returned her *A Wrinkle in Time* manuscript. This ultimate rejection seemed to carry an unmistakable command: Stop this foolishness and learn to make cherry pie. She recorded this moment of decision: "It didn't matter how small or inadequate my talent. If I never had another book published (after her first one in

1945), and it was very clear to me that this was a real possibility, I still had to write." *A Wrinkle in Time* won the Newbery Award in 1962, and has gone on to sell 10 million copies.

I feel the same way about persisting in developing my writing talent—however small or inadequate it is. Writing is challenging, hard work. In some way that is difficult to explain to people who don't like to write, that for me to be who I'm meant to be means that I write.

Now that I have plans for solitude and uninterrupted thinking time, I find myself put upon and impatient when others invade with their needs and wants. I've learned that instead of acting the martyr, I can express my desires and set a boundary around the quiet time I need for this introspective work. I want to balance this with my desire to contribute and be an influence for good.

The Workaholic: I come from a long line of industrious people, so I learned that I have value especially when I'm productive. The more I do, the better. Pride comes from efficiently fitting something extra—a project, a service—into the cracks until each day bursts at the seams. As I grew into adulthood I found myself consumed with work, family responsibilities, and community involvement. I became addicted to work and the "high" of accomplishment and productivity.

I would take on more and more, without evaluating whether I had the energy and desire. There was always more to do than I could accomplish, and I stayed tired all the time. Exhaustion and burnout were my rewards, and no one could accuse me of not doing enough. Even so it seems that an empty spot remained, or something was missing.

When I die from doing too much, maybe then I'll finally *be* enough.

The shadow side of workaholism is the belief that apart from productivity and efficiency, I'll never be enough. Instead of accepting the truth that I am enough without the trappings of overdoing, I'm like a greyhound chasing an illusionary rabbit around a racetrack. The outer self is destroyed because the inner self is never accepted or trusted or seen as whole already. The unspoken message I've had to release is, "You must always be productive so that others don't see you as lazy!"

I'm reminded of a lecture I attended a few years ago. Sue Bender shared her experience of working with Kevin, a potter who broke and then mended his pots before selling them. As she cracked her own pot and gathered up every piece and shard to rebuild her creation, she realized that it was a metaphor of her own self and that she was whole already—all the pieces were there, everything she needed to work with to be her true self. I thought of all of the pieces of myself and marveled that until I heard her tell her story that I had thought I had to fill some missing piece with productivity.

The strongest impression I've had since slowing down has been to add play into my life. With play there is no time constraint or expectations of results. I'm intentional and fully present in the moment. There are no deadlines, no expectation of completing something for someone else; just the pleasure of the experience for myself. This adjustment into the flow of play has proven difficult because I've had half a century plus of time-filled responsibility and an imagination full of things to accomplish.

I'm learning to invest in the notion that

meaning and acceptance come from who we are, not how much we do. I review the underlying message and reframe: What are more healthy motivations? How can my inner light and my own natural rhythm rather than others' expectations guide me?

The Warrior surfaced again recently during a massage therapy session. The image of battle armor came to both the therapist's and my mind as she tried to loosen the rock-solid tightness in my shoulders. I probably started figuratively wearing armor in the early 80s the first time we struggled financially in our marriage. Developing a marketable skill was essential and it was several years before that became a possibility. It seemed as though I was continually fighting against financial insecurity.

If I could only define and then control all the parameters of my family's financial life

I would feel secure. I did everything I could to keep uncertainty at bay, especially by staying frightfully busy. Nevertheless, uncertainty and thus fear of anything I couldn't control have been companions through most of my married life with an entrepreneur, who thrives on taking financial business risks.

The shadow side I'm always battling is scarcity thinking. Albert Einstein said that the most important decision to make is whether we believe the universe is friendly or hostile. Scarcity thinking tells me it is not friendly; possibility thinking says yes. Scarcity thinking says stay small in your comfort zone; possibility thinking says stretch into the unknown.

Unless I was working full time and contributed some income, I slipped easily into flight mode—a feeble attempt to avoid feeling that life was uncontrollable. Then I didn't have to reconcile the part of my psyche that could possibly make peace with uncertainty. To acknowledge that uncertainty is the reality, requires that instead of hitting my head and heart against the wall and complaining, "This isn't it," time and time again, I open up to how I can experiment with it. I can apply a new set of principles by asking new questions and testing old assumptions:

- What's surprising? What have I learned?
- What is different from what I expected that has opened new opportunities?
- How can I look at uncertainty as a gift—as a pathway into a thriving environment?

Recently I've moved on from my university-working years. And now because of an abrupt drying up of monthly funds, I have an opportunity to revisit this tendency to re-armor myself and review what residual thinking patterns are keeping me stuck in the notion that I have to work my heart to death to keep uncertainty at bay. It's an old habit that is no longer useful and creates tension in my neck and shoulders, as if I'm shouldering battle armor—something I have to emotionally put on and equally important, can remove. There is enough and to spare.

My authentic self, full of light and love, shines in those places where I still have residual pockets of ego (fear, resistance, driven behavior) that need clearing. I'm ready, open and not resistant, so I don't step away or numb myself when the work I need to do stretches me. I lean in, fully present, trusting, and tell the truth. I open myself to the lessons to be learned, stay congruent, keep my heart pliable, and listen for the still, inner voice speaking quietly from the center of my being. I'm moving into that place of clarity, deep listening, breathing, and plenty of quiet space—drenching myself in possibility. These questions arise and different questions may come to you:

- How will I nurture my soul?
- How will I care for the introverted little girl who found such pleasure in spending time alone?
- What is my need for solitude and alone time telling me?
- Who am I in the deepest recesses of my being?
- How will I embrace uncertainty and thrive?
- What process leads to an openness of spirit, a deep inner wisdom, and enlightenment?
- What has to die for me to move forward?
- What images form my collage, and what messages do the shadow sides offer?

What happens at midlife
is an unraveling—a time when the desperate pull
to live the life you want becomes stronger than
the one you're "supposed" to live.

You are challenged by the universe to strip away
what is disingenuous in your nature.
Release any barriers
to the expression of your true self.

Discover what makes you happy.
Include yourself in the circle of your caring.
Selt-trust becomes anchored in the belief that
you are enough . . .
—adapted from Brene Brown

Chapter 5
Descent

"Women find their way back to them-
selves not by moving up and out into the light
like men, but by moving down into the depths
of the ground of their being."
—Maureen Murdock

I am my only companion on this inner, soul-searching journey. Even though I
feel that descent, whatever that is, is necessary and unhurried, I have some concerns
about taking time for myself, and am tempted
to label any personal introspective time as
self-indulgent or self-centered. I learned early
to criticize and analyze my motives as an important part of intellectual maturity. The critic
in my mind, that involuntary and repetitive

voice, urged me to shun the uncertainty that could come with introspection. Eckhart Tolle explains, "The core of the ego is unconsciousness. We keep the ego strong with habitual and unconscious complaining, reacting, blaming, comparing and judging; we stay in victim mode." Consequently, developing self-trust stays at the bottom of my never ending to-do list.

Growing self-trust seems to be a process, and I'm descending deeper into the soil of my soul, into myself, to encourage the tender seeds of self-trust to thrive. I have gained some of this inner assurance through experience. I've trusted myself more and more as life presented dilemmas. Now I'm being pulled toward trusting myself in a new way.

To become comfortable and at ease with my authentic self, my soul self, just as I am, without the trappings and insecurities of the world, I must sort through the patterns of my thoughts and feelings. Observation is the key. I notice the hue and flow of emotions and ideas without judgment. These seem to come in unexpected and random spurts: grief, rage, resistance, and confusion, interspersed with moments of gratitude for where I am at this stage of life. I remind myself to become "centered in self," where I take the seasonal opportunity to gain insight.

I slow my breathing and notice the feelings in my gut that lead me toward the calming peace that sustains me in the tension of not knowing. Often it is my tendency to imagine the worst that ties my stomach in knots. I recognize the difference and choose to step into possibilities and solutions rather than become numb or give up.

Descent is an inner conduit into the interior I touch when I give myself a full measure of the alone time I'm craving. It's a pathway of luxurious wandering and of being myself and with myself, without the compulsion of doing all the time. Over the past few years, it's become more urgent to move into this place of being. It's where I say, "Stop!" It's where I inspect the underside of the tapestry of my life—the beginnings and endings of earlier decisions and experiences. It's time for me to make some new choices. In this space of my inner journey, I've identified three concepts that foster my ability to trust my inner self. These include: attentiveness, full acceptance, and a willingness to engage intuition.

As children, we are born with these gifts, and gradually exchange them for a worldview of self, full of criticism and doubt. We often hold back for fear of making a mistake or not being good enough. Gradually these negative patterns of perspective obscure or overshadow the qualities of our true nature. In addition, they block the process of self-rediscovery so essential in midlife.

• • •

Everything in this world carries an energy vibration, including our thoughts and emotions. They flow from us in electromagnetic waves, automatically attracting identical frequencies. Each of us has developed habitual patterns of thinking and feeling. We are often unaware of the energy expended through the expression of our thoughts and emotions and how these vibrations influence our circumstances. As a result, most of us are all over the place—happy one minute and worried or fractured the next.

Thoughts and feelings that project low vibrational frequencies include shame, toxic guilt, anger, worry, frustration, anxiety, thinking there's never enough, doubt, and resentment. These lead me into a downward spiral of fear and resistance, and into a place of not trusting myself. Harville Hendrix writes, "Energy follows attention. Every time we invest in the negative (It's not working, I'm not good enough, perfect enough . . .) we are honing our ability to detect faults. Our energy amplifies the annoying and we create the conditions that allow our problems to grow like weeds in an unkempt field."

In earlier times and even once in a while now, I resist changing my thinking because I want to believe that outward circumstances and people cause my frustrations, problems, and distress. Resistance often surfaces in unconscious phrases that focus on what I can't do, can't control, or should do. When I use complaining, blaming, and rationalization as problem solving techniques, these block options and desires. I'm attentive to how my body feels when these unconscious forms manifest themselves as holding back.

If I do carry negative patterns of thinking, neurons in my heart, such as my tendency toward extreme worry or ruminating, that is where the house cleaning must begin. Sometimes, unexpectedly I stumble back into an old habit. I call this overcaring, a term used by authors, Doc Childre and Howard Martin: "The draining cycle of overcare begins as we over-identify with a situation, issue, or person we care about, because we get over-attached to how we want things to turn out." True care reduces stress for the sender and the receiver. When my care for someone is giving me stress or anxiety, I realize I have crossed a line into overcare that is an energy drain. I move out of my mind and into my heart. I breathe love and appreciation into my heart and immerse my disturbing feelings in the compassionate intelligence of my heart.

Sometimes I refuse to do the work. Usually I'm exhausted, and when this happens, I've learned to wait until I'm rested. When I'm ready, I work on one negative thought or phrase at a time. I practice changing the negative into its positive opposite, which holds a higher vibration. When my scarcity belief script—there's never enough— takes over my thinking, for instance, I practice using the following phrase, "There is enough and to spare" until it becomes second nature. Many times I search for the phrase or wording that works before I can practice in such a way that alters my perceptions of the world around me.

The surprising insight I have gained is that new and unexpected circumstances test my resolve to stay in tune with my inner light and generate positive emotions that carry high vibrational frequencies. These include peace, joy, gratitude, optimism, enthusiasm, generosity, and unconditional love. These encourage me toward possibility, even in the face of difficulty or challenge. These emotions bring "light" into the darkness of my interior journey when I feel lost.

• • •

It seems that accepting myself has always come with exceptions: "Yes I like myself, except for . . ." I stopped liking myself early in junior-high. That's when I began to compare myself to others and noticed that I always fell short in one way or another. I focused on what I didn't like about myself.

Coming to a place of full acceptance means that I release myself from the bondage of self-criticism and putdowns. It means overhauling the expectations I have for myself, and softening them into preferences. For one thing, I quit should-ing on myself. I don't carry an exhaustive list of shoulds swirling in my mind, but there is an underbelly—any number of things to be accomplished that I never get around to doing.

We burden our children and ourselves with too much to do. If these extras are on our list of shoulds indefinitely, chances are high that we are never going to love doing them, and thus they will remain undone, weighing us down, and keeping us in a guilt ridden state of mind.

In order to change this, I un-shoulder the list of shoulds and review them realistically to determine which ones I can release, especially the ones that make me feel drained or frustrated. Usually these are the uber-extras on my plate that I believe I should be able to fit into my already busy life. I shift to what I can do and what I want to do, let go of the rest or delegate them to someone else.

Several times while I was working full time, I had the opportunity as an instructional writer to develop state curriculum projects. Each time, this was extra on my plate, and I juggled my life to squeeze in the intensity of inventive writing. One year was particularly hectic. Besides my administrative assignment, the extra university course I was teaching, and the curriculum project I'd committed to, my husband and I were chasing three of four teenagers around to high school sporting events along with the regular weekly obligations. These teenagers were so busy they began to neglect their house cleaning assignments at home. My husband traveled extensively to trade shows and wasn't around to pitch in either.

When I expressed my frustration several evenings in a row, he eventually suggested we hire someone to clean the house for the rest of the school year until I had completed the curriculum project.

"Hire someone!" I exclaimed. "I couldn't do that."

It was horrifying to think that I couldn't fit it all in and would find myself in need of extra help outside our family. The trouble was that I couldn't do it all. I was six months into the project and exhausted before I finally gave myself permission to hire a cleaning service without feeling guilty. The last six months of the project became less stressful because I wasn't trying to do everything at home and work by myself.

Peter London writes, "As long as we feel we are inadequate, insufficient, we will rely on others to provide orientation, definition, and purpose for our life." Self-acceptance also means I let go of the expectations and crit-

icisms that others burden me with, usually
out of misplaced concern. Every transition is
heavy-laden with shoulds.

I sat with a friend who surprised me by
severely criticizing a choice I recently made,
laying out her view of the consequences and
advising me away from my decision. I felt
unjustly attacked and could have responded
with defensiveness and excuses. As I paused
to gather myself before I responded, an insight
came into my mind: Her words had nothing to
do with me, rather with herself. Since it didn't
make sense to her, surely it wasn't right for
me. She projected her fears onto me. A sense
of confidence filled my being and confirmed
my decision. I didn't absorb her objections or
try to control or change her opinion. Rather
than react, I reaffirmed that the timing was
right for me and expressed my appreciation
for her concern, closing the conversation. I

was free to stand for myself and validate my decision in an appropriate moment.

When I'm willing to be in this introspective process of self-trust, I'm not defensive as I listen to others' ideas and concerns. I listen more conscientiously to those that rise from my heart. I feel a sense of inner peace because I let go of control. I detach from others' opinions and judgments that are offered in what they think are in my best interest. Linear time becomes less important than being congruent with myself in the moment. Kathleen Brehony says, "We live in a culture that does not honor inner work. Like a riptide, this process requires surrender rather than control—allowing ourselves to come to a place of not knowing— trusting the integrity of our own inner process, the wisdom of self, and our own strength."

One of the ways I measure how well I trust myself is that I quit explaining the de-

tails of what I'm doing to everyone I know
so they can offer a critique. When I change
the way I'm doing things, often some friend
or family member shows up with objections.
Instead of offering a long explanation, I use a
simple phrase like, "I'm doing this now because it's the best timing," or, "It's a good time
for me to grow." I know I am moving toward
full acceptance when I let go of being all things
to all people, of focusing solely on my faults,
and begin to appreciate and respect who I've
become and the strengths I've developed over
a lifetime.

What are those strengths? They are my
unique and enduring talents. I notice these
when I identify the activities that bring me
the greatest satisfaction and I focus on those.
An inner voice encourages me forward; its
messages remind me to be compassionate,
patient, and generous to myself, as well as

others. I also courageously face the subtle suggestions for change that keep me in touch with my authentic self. Ironically, amid the uncertainty and confusion I face in this descent, I begin to see the light within that has always existed, offering assurance and direction constantly and without fail.

• • •

As I track through journaling for what has changed for me over the years, I can see the biggest transformations have come through what I've learned about my thinking and my heart—how I sort through things and move ideas and projects forward, what happens when I feel stopped in my progress, and how I deal with anger or disappointment. I see where I've learned to be curious or patient, and what I've learned about my true nature in times of crisis, or in the face of others' criticism.

It's my need for certainty that silences
this intuitive voice. When I'm urged to be patient, and I resist rushing about checking out
my frustrations with others, I'm gifted with a
sense of calm. It is then that I become sensitive to the internal signposts along the way
that were previously unnoticed.

I'm intuitive when I'm not analytical
or forcing an outcome. Instead, I let the answers come to me. An exercise that engages
my intuitive voice is writing 100 questions
without stopping. This helps me see the variety and depth of thoughts in my mind. The
first questions are always practical. In my
life, that usually has to do with gardening or
remembering birthdays. After 30-40 questions
though, themes and patterns begin to emerge.
I see what I'm passionate about, what I've forgotten that I love to do, and what I've put off
that needs attention.

My deepest insights always come toward the end of my list. These often surprise me, and I know I'm accessing my heart wisdom. I study my list to identify themes, which I underline in different colors of ink. I highlight the dreams and desires that surface. I continue asking questions such as these from Peter London that access the knowledge that comes to me through an inner vision:

- How high have I allowed my imagination to soar?
- How much sweep and scope have I permitted myself?
- How deep, how honest, how full are the steps I'm willing to take?

At this point I pause, reflective and curious. I come to the center of my mind. I hold the candle of insight high in the air in front of me. I imagine doors leading into numerous rooms full of past memories. Some doors are open and the rooms full of light, and I know I have done the requisite work of forgiveness and healing and released the negative impact of past experiences. I'm searching for the shadow places where cobwebs and dust have accumulated in the corners—the parts of my personal story—a net of beliefs that I've been unwilling to give up that hold me back from moving forward. Once I'm mindful of my stream of consciousness, I release any residue of self-criticism and reclaim my curiosity, intuition, and creativity.

At one time or another, I have experienced a moment of clarity and flow that comes when what I'm doing seems exactly right. My heart and mind register contentment. I've had this happen with work assignments and personally in creative moments—when I've accompanied someone on the piano, when I shared an original idea with a group that clarified a concept for them, when I'm rocking an exhausted and grumpy grandchild, when a story or paragraph writes itself. In these moments, time stops—timelines and pressing obligations fade away. I know exactly how to respond. I'm not second-guessing my choices or motives. I rejoice in the process. I move deeply into the sacred space of knowing myself and trusting that I will choose, learn, and influence others with integrity.

Elisabeth Kubler-Ross writes, "People are like stained-glass windows. They sparkle and shine when the sun is out, but when the darkness sets in their beauty is revealed only if there is a light from within." Now when I stand in that place of peace and clarity, I recognize a steady light that does not flicker or go out when the fierce winds and storms of life seem to combine against me. I am sustained and eager. What about you?

ARE YOU LISTENING TO YOUR HEART?

IT'S TELLING YOU
WHAT YOU'RE MEANT-
TO BE DOING . . .

Chapter 6
The Room in the Middle

*"If we never pause long enough to know
the silence, how will we know what possibilities it contains?"*
—Sue Bender

I've been muddling around in these
inner journey stages for several years since
my resistance to "the call" into stillness. It
reminds me of the back and forth of the grief
cycle of denial, anger, bargaining, depression,
and acceptance. The steps into my personal
journey have been uneven, as if I'm descending into the lower levels of a medieval castle.
Some steps are manageable; others are steep
or slippery. And I've had to move through this

at a slower, unhurried pace than how I usually manage things.

As I approach this metaphorical room in the middle that is mine alone, I'm reminded that time off, time out, time for quiet reflection doesn't usually happen as an accepted part of life. Neither parents nor culture taught me to access a refuge of inner calm, or search for the deeper roots of my pains and desires within myself. Society does not value contemplation or space for downtime, although for some, meditation and prayer are common practices. My impression is that this place of stillness is not going to be accessed when I can stop everything for any length of time. It will be a place I discover or rediscover in the eye of the hurricane of challenges, sorrows, and blessings that surround my life. The pace of living increases as easily as freeway speeds.

The technology that allows me to stay

connected at cruise control speed to cell
phone, fax, computer, answering machine, etc.
unrelentingly drives our fast paced society.
These "life-enhancing" super-tech improve-
ments and social constructs catapult our
biorhythms into overdrive. I easily keep my
life as busy as a video game or action-packed
movie. I'm in sync or entrained with the pulse
of technology—a constant, untiring rhythm
that is faster than the average heartbeat. It's
similar to what happens when two out-of-sync
pendulum clocks sit next to each other. By the
next day they are keeping time together.

I still crowd my life, forgetting that
things are noticed and appreciated more
when they're surrounded by space—breathing room—instead of being so tightly-bunched
together that I feel only the burden of an
over-filled life. I remember a particular session
I had some time ago with an acupuncturist.

After discussing what was ailing me, he mentioned that it would be good for me to create some breathing space around the whirl of my thoughts, and my tendency to over think the complexities in my life. It seemed strange at the time. Now it resonates.

The quiet must go on for more than a few minutes of solitude in order to come to a place where I can listen for and begin to trust my own sense of inner knowing. My first experience with time off occurred when my husband took the kids to visit his family in Texas for Thanksgiving and left me home alone. I was exhausted from the semester's work. A 13-hour drive to Texas and back sounded even more tiring. Instead I thought, I would lie in bed and relax—no meals to fix, clothes to wash, children to taxi around, or work assignments to complete. They left Tuesday evening and would return late Sunday night.

The next morning I slept in until 8 a.m., ate breakfast, and sat on the sofa reading, when I realized I could wash all the bed sheets while I relaxed. After I put the first batch of sheets in the washer, I chose to reorganize the linen closets. I noticed several bills to pay, got those in the mail, and pulled a few weeds near the driveway as I walked back to the house. I decided that the patio needed sweeping before any snow arrived. After a late lunch, I thought I might take a nap. Instead I wrote a couple of letters and sewed a quilt top for an expectant mother in my neighborhood.

By the time Sunday came I had moved the furniture and vacuumed around all the baseboards in every room of the house. The experience reminded me of a quote from a calendar I've kept:

"I have nearly killed myself with my compulsive housekeeping. There's always something that needs to be done. Recently, we moved to the mountains and my husband thought I would, at least, be relieved of such extensive yard work. But after I got the house the way I wanted, I found myself wanting to tidy up the forest."

One winter day we were traveling in the dreary part of the drive along I-40 through northern New Mexico. The frosty backdrop of dry pale, yellowed grass faded into the nondescript gray color of the bluffs in the distance, as if God forgot his paintbrush during this eruptive stage of creation. The word "bleak" came to mind. What hides deep beneath the seemingly barren landscape of a life stopped for a moment? I'm carried forward reluctantly on the winds of change and because I don't like the landing strip I see, I hover above, tiring easily. I stay aloft, and feel out of sorts, unadjusted, and restless.

I stay quiet in the car for a long while, and the next insight shocks me. The surprising resistance to changing my life comes from unspoken family expectations of my youth that entangle and trip up my intentions:

* Keep working, don't stop, be produc tive, and make a difference.

* Work all the time and work hard enough, only then will good things happen.

* Keep going as fast as you can, or you'll get behind and never catch up.

These fear based belief scripts are internalized perceptions about what I'm supposed to do or not do. When I recognize the harm these unconscious messages may cause, I can change the ones holding me back to others more accurate and useful. "If this belief script isn't true, what possibilities open to my view?"

Others may have different unconscious messages rattling around in their core, but may also discover as I have, that a little extra inner work needs to be completed around these few residual, limiting assumptions I've decided must be deeply etched in my DNA. I can bring them to the surface and reframe or release them.

• • •

I was out of town for a few days visiting my mother-in-law and had bracketed some time for writing this chapter. I found an isolated spot on a wooden bench off the café in a local bookstore where I could sit at a table, searching my thoughts for something about quiet and stillness. I was reminded of a line from *The Alchemist* by Paulo Coelho, the story of a young shepherd boy named Santiago who travels from his homeland in Spain to the Egyptian desert in search of a treasure. I checked the book to find the quote: "Relaxed and unhurried, he resolves to walk through the narrow streets. Only in that way would he be able to read the omens." The following questions surfaced:

- How do I change from busy and in overdrive to relaxed and unhurried?
- How will I recognize the signs that come from inside, from my intuitive soul?
- Where will I direct my passion?
- What must go away to allow for regeneration time?

It was during a trip to Madrid, Spain one hot summer to study Spanish for two weeks that I accidently discovered my natural rhythm. I was far from home and my long list of things to accomplish. Each morning after breakfast we would walk half a mile from the dorms to our classroom, attend classes until noon, and then walk home for lunch. Instead of daily excursions with dozens of exuberant young and rowdy students, I took an hour to leisurely meander and explore the streets by myself. I would buy a piece of fruit and a pastry for a snack, and then settle into the dorm's downstairs lounge to study, write, and nap. That room was always empty and much cooler than my un-air conditioned dorm room on the fourth floor. No one disturbed me. I ate an early dinner and with no television, I was usually in bed by 8:30 p.m. I began to slow down and rest, probably for the first time in my life.

It's a dramatic shift to move from overdoing to my natural rhythm, which I've found in musical terms, is andante—about the speed of a slow walk; just a little slower than my standing heart rate—much slower than the constant beat of technology. I knew it would not be easy to maintain once I returned to my

family and work, although the shift in speed
and the quiet I experienced untangled me for
some time afterward.

The trick is to connect with my natural
rhythm when everything conspires against
me. I operate so well at full throttle and never
learned how to downshift. On a daily basis,
this means that I stop during the busy day
and take a breather: I sit on my deck with
a cup of herbal tea and soak in the morning sun. I play the piano or curl into a comfy
chair, read a chapter in a book, and then close
my eyes for ten minutes or so. I take time to
moodle—Brenda Ueland's invented word. She
writes,

> "The imagination needs moodling: long,
> inefficient, happy idling, dawdling, and
> puttering. These people who are always
> briskly doing something and as busy as
> waltzing mice, they have little, sharp,

staccato ideas, such as saving ten cents on a Sunday's roast. But they have no slow, big ideas. And the fewer consoling, noble, shining, free, jovial, magnanimous ideas that come, the more desperately they rush and run."

When the opportunity arises during a trip to California, I break away. I'm sitting on a granite rock in the Sequoia National Forest letting thoughts and ideas rise to the surface. I track my breathing, and still the urge to write the next to-do list that presses for visibility and action. The vista stretches out in front of me for hundreds of miles. Lavender-shadowed hills on the edge of the horizon blend into the pale clear blue sky. The only sound comes from a woodpecker in the distance. Time feels ancient and slow moving in this spot. The elements have no agenda except to be. I settle in, feeling the coolness of the air and the warmth of the sun, and breathe more slowly.

I wander in the wilderness of my life for a time, although I'm not lost. I'm just loosening the edges of responsibility I've carried for so many years, as if I'm unpicking the seams of a well-stitched vest that needs altering. It feels strange and good—certainly transitory: uncertain with moments of clarity and something else that surprises me: abounding gratitude. I settle deep into this place of stillness where I experience constant peace, balance, and calm in the midst of my busy life.

• • •

After decades of marching to continuous to-do lists, the "why" and "how" of stillness eluded me for a long time. I'm at a loss without a to-do list, and forgetful. Any effort to quiet my mind seemed futile and tiresome. I've been ungraceful at this ever since, like a child learning to ride a bicycle for the first time and toppling to the ground with each effort. Time and time again, life with all its many agendas takes over and the plan for deep quiet fades. I found Brene Brown's definition of stillness clarifying: "Stillness is not about focusing on nothingness; it's about creating a clearing. It's opening up an emotionally clutter-free space and allowing ourselves to feel and think and dream and question."

Coming to the insight that stillness can bring does require practice and more than motionlessness. It's a willingness to calm a mind that has a tendency to race ahead, over-thinking, analyzing—seeking certainty and control, thus avoiding the present moment where calm resides. It's a quietness of being.

One day, stillness beckoned me to create some space around my thinking. Uncertainty pushed it away. As I paused to un-

derstand my resistance, I had an "aha" moment: Busyness kept me distracted from an
underlying sense of fear: What if I can't figure
out what I'm supposed to do next? The unspoken message is that I always have to have an
agenda, a goal I'm striving toward; in fact, an
abundance of goals with details to keep track
of all at once. I'm impatient with my own evo-
lution, which seems to continually twist and
turn in unexpected ways.

In that moment I embrace the uncertainty by letting go of unanswerable "what if .
. ." questions. I hold the tension of not knowing, of dilemmas with no actual solutions or
moving parts. I let my time of quiet fill with
acceptance—no complaining, no resisting—a
kind of surrender into a place with no agenda
or expectation; a space where questions could
arise without having to know any of the answers. When the stillness is unnerving, I tune

into my heartbeat, constant and true, amazing as the star in my soul that shines through me, and flood my being with compassion.

Yes, some of my best times for stillness and entering into inner silence and reflection come when I can totally unhook from all that I enjoy immensely—responsibilities and projects that are always jostling for attention like little children. Even in the face of too much good, I gradually become dried out. Inner solitude allows for "times of seasoning" where I hone my ability to synthesize the experiences and changes that occur within before moving on. I move out of the fray of frantic busyness and into calmer waters where I become a wiser, more integrated, and authentic being. I pace myself and create healthy boundaries that protect my stamina. My time in the room in the middle increases my interior resiliency— my ability to rebound and adjust as life continually surprises me.

• • •

Fallow time refers to cultivated land that has been plowed and left idle without sowing for a season or more. I grew up on a farm in Wyoming where I saw first hand the land sometimes left without any crops growing on it because the soil shows signs of exhaustion. There is space that surrounds my need to lay fallow for the most part—like a field that needs a rest from planting for a season—until I can gain some clarity about what is most important to move forward. So I bundle up—breathe the fresh mountain air and sit for a time.

I had the luxury of calling my time away from the university a few years ago "a sabbatical." I was writing full time and focused. It felt productive and meaningful. Now, a few years distant from that scheduled space, I find I'm not ready for retirement nor can I borrow the university's "time away" term once more. Why is it so difficult to admit that I may be starving for some moodling time—space unfilled and uncluttered with things to do, projects, goals, or assignments? Those unspoken expectations rise to the surface again: Keep working! I release them into the universe in metaphorical helium balloons.

I'm in stasis—like the snow in a frozen winter scene before spring melts it away. I'm inside a chrysalis where the initial structures of my life are breaking down completely so new ones can form. There is a reorganization going on in my deepest self. There is also a steady inner light in the darkness.

A season of play beckons me, interspersed with physical nurturing and rest. Perhaps I could say, "yes," only to those things that would nurture and heal. In that moment I

relax and free my mind and heart from expectations. I let the silence—these moments
of waiting, of fertile emptiness feed me. I sort
through messages I've been receiving for the
past several years and have sorely neglected,
namely to quiet my mind and listen to my
heart. In this place of transition where I'm
searching for answers to unspoken and unknown, yet real questions, I stretch my heart
into quiet moments where silence and stillness
are my friends. I soften the edges of my heart
and sit without any concern for schedules or
projects. Here are some insightful questions:

• What assumptions am I still not
aware I'm making?

• What might I now invent that I haven't yet invented that would give me
other choices?

• What kind of nurturing and creativity
do I want in the next part of my life?

I want to invent a life that stays connected to this spacious room in the middle—this center place of nurturing, softness, and calm. It is mine alone to cultivate. It's a private garden where I can retreat from the relentless pace of outer life.

I am willing to make the ungainly transition from the pace of racing greyhounds to a more sedate and healthy state. It's living my life from the inside out—letting this sense of tranquility permeate all that I do. Henry Ward Beecher says, "There are joys which long to be ours. God sends ten thousand truths, which come about like birds seeking inlet, but we are shut up to them [in our busy lives], so they bring us nothing, but sit and sing a while upon the roof, and then fly away."

There are moments when the world
becomes still and the most pressing
thing to do is nothing—
Gaze in wonder at the beauty
around you.
Close your eyes, breathe deeply,
and rest, rest, rest.

There will be rest, and sure stars
shining. I will make this world of my
own devising.
I shall find the crystal of peace,
—above me stars I shall find.
—from Sara Teasdale

Chapter 7
Shedding

"The healthier we are, the less time we spend denying our needs."
—Marsha Sinetar

I can feel myself stirring, stretching, and thinking in a different way. Even though life is full of the same complications and possibilities, I have a new perspective. I'm expanding my mind and heart into new ideas and reflecting on a different set of questions. I close my eyes and mentally look at the various facets of my life. I can touch the edges of my imagined chrysalis and want to push through into the sunlight. I'm reminded of a baby waking up. The first thing that occurs is a full-body stretch with tiny arms reaching as far as possible above the head.

Since I created a space for this inner journey and contemplation, I have been in stasis for some time. I am getting ready to move, wiggle my toes, and desire especially to stay open to the wisdom of my heart and intuition. The deeper I've gone into the quiet recesses of my soul, the more substantial my true self appears, and the more playful and joyful. The reorganization that's going on inside is rising to the surface, and I'm being asked to radically simplify my life.

I stay curled in on myself a while longer because I know that I must remain patient for a season. What has been newly formed cannot be instantly released. My desires, impressions, and intentions are in embryo and seem fragile. Unless I slowly and consciously integrate this new awareness of myself, old habits and

attitudes will show up over and over again. I'm
not redefining myself; instead I'm un-defining
myself, as if I'm gifting myself a blank sheet
of watercolor paper on which to imagine and
create a new and healthier self-image.

I've been in the process of doing just
that lately: erasing or dissolving everything I
know about me except my core—those ima-
ginal discs in the chrysalis that are not destroyed when the caterpillar digests itself.
Those discs use the protein-rich soup all
around them to form the different parts of the
adult butterfly. My "discs" of curiosity, loving
kindness, generosity, creativity, resiliency,
and desire to continually learn will stay with
me.

I'm letting go of the roles, the importance of visibility at the university level, of
being overly productive and exhausted, and
the expectations of others for what I'm to do

in this next stage of life. In addition, I'm examining all my extra stuff I've accumulated in our home over the years: dozens and dozens of books, boxes and drawers full of papers, curriculum and other instructional projects, fabric, the paraphernalia left over from earlier interests, puzzles, and games, etc.

Then there are the dregs of old hurtful feelings of resentment, fear, anger, and sorrow—those particles stuck to the bottom of the barrel that plague me to a lesser degree now. I can feel that these need to be gently scraped away. I would like to un-encumber even more, although I cling to a few projects that remain to be completed before my life could be as simple as I envision.

For the past year, the message to myself has been, "nothing else yet." Except for things that are directly related to my few goals of unencumbering, writing, and contribution, I have been resisting all the luscious or enticing projects that pass in front of me. Even so, my mind stays restless. It distracts me from what I must face that is unknown or unresolved because the expectation to work all the time is still so ingrained in me. I "see" so many things I want to do and could do. Why not do only the things I love to do?

I feel unsettled and ungrounded and must learn how to anchor myself in spite of uncertainty. I observe any tightness brought on by an underlying sense of fear and its unhelpful questions: "What if I can't figure this out?" "What if I fail?" These types of questions are unanswerable and I breathe out and release them. The relaxation response—a state of calm produced by breathing and meditation—actually switches the genes that are related to augmenting our immune system. I ground myself by breathing in gratitude and

I breathe appreciation and kindness into my adrenals, the part of my body that suffers the most when I tense up or become exhausted.

It's in the space, the pauses, and the silence that I regenerate and recharge. I know I must continue learning to be quiet and deeply attentive often during the day, to listen to my soul's urges. These differ from the shoulds of the mind. By shifting into curiosity, I reframe uncertainty as an acceptable and trusted friend, and it transforms into increased aliveness and creativity. My plan is to keep gentleness and self-trust and compassion running through my body with each breath. I work slow periods into my days. My calm mind becomes a treasure chest of new questions:

- What does my restless mind say about me?
- Can I embrace the new without needing to control the outcome?

• What fosters meaning for me?

•How can I renew and regenerate
myself?

The process of re-inventing myself at
a slower pace reminds me of how tied I am to
time and accomplishments, and the belief that
"slow" equates with being lazy. I'm reframing
slow as mindful, thoughtful, and filled with
generosity. My heart knows deep down that
my mind and body still crave space that is
restful. Eckhart Tolle notes, "Our lives are one
thing after another, one thought after another,
one worry after another without space. Without space it is difficult to touch the spiritual
dimension." I imagine enough time to accomplish what I want with ease. When I believe
there is enough time and to spare, time ex-
pands into its fullness. I'm engaged in the moment and what's taking place, neither anxious
about getting enough done nor worried about

moving faster than my own natural rhythm.

I moved into hyper drive one morning for a couple of hours of shopping, planting, and to finish piecing a quilt top. Then I detached myself from a schedule, timetable, and list, and decelerated to where I could tap into the slower waves of time. I stopped and observed the bees in the bellflowers and smiled with surprise as a portly bumblebee moved in and out of the tiny spirea blossoms. I relaxed into the sun and shade and deeper breathing of being rather than doing. Allowing myself to transition from a higher to a lower speed has been a helpful practice I want to continue.

I've become resistant to a to-do list, although I write short ones on 3x5 cards because I do want to remember to get some things done and the bills have to be paid on time. Stacked-up books and projects wait in the wings of my days. Which ones will I release? Part of me is just observing, letting my mind drift. As I'm glancing through magazines, I find images and phrases that capture my attention. I rip these out for creating a new vision board. I remind myself that when I'm waiting, I'm not being slothful. Instead, I'm developing a different muscle of attentiveness—one filled with grace and gratitude. I'm doing the most important thing at this stage of life: learning how to let my soul lead.

There is an outer life overfilled with expectations, responsibilities and obligations: school, career and jobs, family, home, and community. There is also an inner life; one that includes my thoughts about life, my perceptions, how I respond—whether with resistance or openness, the assumptions I make, my stream of consciousness, how I create or envision, what attitudes keep me stuck, and what I can change. Attention to this inner life and its beckoning voice must become more than an inconsistent exercise if I'm to move successfully from the confines of my metaphorical chrysalis.

I also want a creative outlet, and writing fills this currently. To develop new ideas is to move into the unknown, to awaken buried perceptions, to be alive and free without worrying about the result. In this process, there's no right or wrong way. There is only the next step, the next experiment, the next moment of listening. To hear the voice of the creator within I must learn to recognize the signs, dreams, visions, and feelings I receive; mostly feelings.

I know there is a river of calm strength and harmony flowing through my center. I want to create the next 5-year plan and yet I feel so much of my life hovers in a holding pattern that I'm willing to let that rest a while longer. I'm in a place of reflection in which

there is no time frame—no sunrise or sun-
set—just dim understanding. I'm not sure
of the seasons or cycles in this space. Just
that I must have time to think and not think.
I need space around my thinking. My mind
is over-stimulated—around and responsible
for enough people and obligations that I'm
still drained most of the time. I need plenty of
downtime.

Even though things are the same, I
have a new perspective. The last thing that
needs to happen before I leave the chrysalis
is to establish new boundaries around my
health and well-being. I am willing to explore
what priorities will allow my heart full rein in
my life. So when I imagine some direction I
want to go, or some project I want to take on,
I pause and let my heart lead. I'm learning to
manage my energy levels, which means that
less will be accomplished and this is a strug-

gle for me. I can ask—

- What's still missing that I want more of in my life?
- What needs to deepen?
- What struggles are insignificant that I can release?
- What signal will I invent when I forget to slow down?

I have come to recognize some blessings of slowness I couldn't have articulated in earlier years. Downtime actually eases my sense of being overwhelmed. It also gives my brain time to make connections that provide insights. When I untether from technology and its buffet of information and things to do and move into a more unstructured space, I find I'm doing my best creative thinking. Authors John Briggs and David Peat tell a story of Bill, a physicist working for a research organization.

"Bill moved a big easy chair into his office. When asked what it was for, he said that he liked to sit and daydream, maybe even sleep a little in the afternoon. The director was horrified, 'You're not paid to sleep; you're supposed to be working all the time you're here.' It didn't help that Bill pointed out that he was publishing far more than his colleagues, and he needed time to daydream in order to come up with new ideas."

I've learned that there is a center space in time that is unhurried and tranquil where I'm able to tap into a place of flow—like the sweet spot on the face of the racquet where I hit my best racquetball shots. It's an intersection of ease and strength where I feel the most relaxed and productive. Once this is a more practiced part of my life I'll be ready to emerge and take flight.

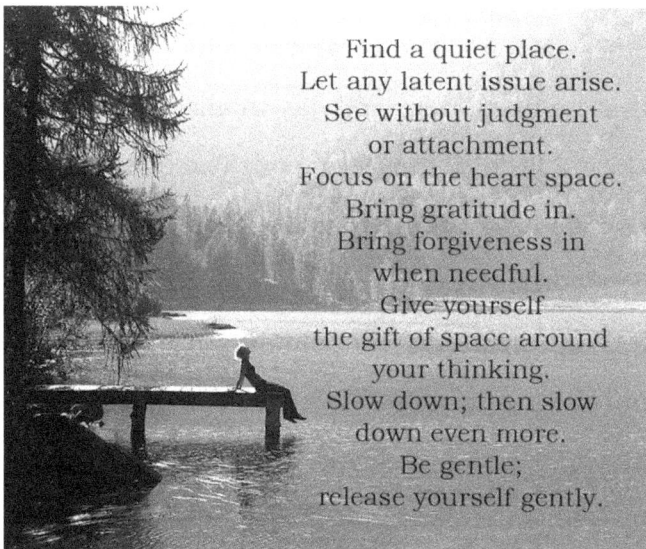

Find a quiet place.
Let any latent issue arise.
See without judgment
or attachment.
Focus on the heart space.
Bring gratitude in.
Bring forgiveness in
when needful.
Give yourself
the gift of space around
your thinking.
Slow down; then slow
down even more.
Be gentle;
release yourself gently.

Chapter 8
Emergence

"Change is frightening, but where there is fear, there's power. If we learn to feel our fear without letting it stop us, fear can become an ally, a signal to tell us that something we have encountered can be transformed."
—Maureen Murdock

My morning began as planned. I rolled out of bed and headed for the gym. For the past three weeks winter has frozen the landscape. The backyard lies in a sea of snow. Even the tree branches have stayed etched with ice crystals. A wave of fog obscures the morning sun, although I can see my breath. This particular morning the air feels different—warmer, almost as if rain would come soon. And it did.

This serves as a metaphor for an inner
life in transition. I've felt numb and frozen at
times, even as I've gone about the daily activities that kept my outer life intact. At some
point a thaw has begun—hardly noticeable,
except that the air surrounding my heart has
changed. No other signal or message appears,
no sudden and noisy crack of ice breaking
through. It's more of a softening, a tender
tendril of hope and clarity emerges, like the
purple crocus that appears through the snow
in late winter, tangible nevertheless. My stops
and starts at stillness and experimentation of
what I want to engage in have created a gentler perspective about the future.

I'm satisfied with the time I've bracketed
for this inner journey over the past several
years. I've discovered important things about
myself as I've wrestled with stillness, especially how deeply I had buried the authentic and

playful parts of my being. I've gained some clarity about emerging from my midlife chrysalis and consider this phase to be a critical stage from which to launch the rest of my life. The most surprising thing I notice as I move from this soul-searching inner journey is the noise—the requests, demands, options, obligations, opinions, and expectations that seem to wait like vultures to eat away at my time. This phase is about space—space to listen, to hear, to be guided. I'm searching for a balance that moves my soul into a life of contentment.

I sense rather than know that this return from descent will require a greater focus and heightened awareness. In fact, as I read others' experiences of this sort, they come away with a commitment to never give away the true self again. My true self invites me toward a balance of work, rest, healing, and play. One strong impression is to pay attention intuitively. Another message coming through is to lighten up.

I've come to the messy phase of experimentation and risk—a time of sorting, dreaming, and remodeling. I've started this on paper first, and then take small steps toward what I would like to do and be and have. This requires a high tolerance for ambiguity. When I'm discovering and deepening the connection to my true self, I feel eager to try on any new set of wings, just so I can say I'm doing something again, rather than have others question my slower than expected progress. I'm reinventing myself, and there's no socially acceptable term for this. I'm like a sailor at sea searching for a port; a dreamer trying to decide which dreams to fulfill, knowing that whichever one I choose will require discipline and effort.

I explain myself in vague terms one day

when a well-meaning friend asks what I'm
doing with all my free time. I hem and haw,
trying to make the uncertainty I'm swimming
through sound like some sophisticated and
scientific experiment. I've found myself caught
up in what Linda Austin terms, "The defensive
use of reality"—dwelling on mundane priorities and events: "I'm helping my spouse with
his aging mother, I'm managing homes and
finances and our yard maintenance"—to keep
myself from telling the truth: it's perfectly fine
for me to take time to figure myself out. It's
just fine for me to be in free fall and unteth-
ered. In fact, until I can be at ease with the
stickiness and lack of visible accomplishment,
I may be like an egg ready to hatch: someone
wants to help me along, and my newly forming
self dies from early exposure.

I'm giving myself a great deal of latitude
for making mistakes. I'm allowing plenty of

time to explore new passions and interests, with permission to play at the process without judgment from others or myself. I learn from my mistakes as well as my successes. That's different than when I was younger and panicked every time I goofed. I've observed that change and transformation are triggered from within. When I trust inner promptings, I chase away the fear of making mistakes, which increases my confidence.

The Biblical creation story reminds me that creating the life I desire proceeds in steps. Clarity is one of the first steps. I love my life, and still yearn for things to happen that I haven't completely identified. I'm still sorting through the puzzle pieces of my existence to figure out what desire or aspiration I want to nurture next. Initially, it's been helpful to brainstorm possible dreams and goals I still want to accomplish.

Wendy Ulrich suggests giving quick answers to the following and then reviewing
those answers to see how they might provide
direction for creative possibilities:

- What five classes would I like to take?
- If I had nine lives, what would I do for
a career in each of them?
- What are five little changes I'd love to
make in my life right now?
- What are three recurring problems I
would like to solve in my personal life?
- What are five questions on any
subject I'd love answers to?
- What three things have I been
worrying about for a long time that
need resolution?
- What is one thing I might explore or
do differently as I consider my answers
to these questions?

• • •

When I step into this experimental phase
of life that I'm inventing (without pay or children to care for), an outlet for my own personal expression, separate from past jobs and
roles, I activate an ancient warning system.
This "guilt" pushes me to shut down my authentic self and adapt to the way of life that
has always been lived by the masses. This is
not the guilt brought on by my doing harm
to others. It is the guilt about what I am—of
failing to be productive enough to have value
in our society.

This compulsion toward adaptability may
come more readily to those who haven't in-
volved themselves in consistent soul searching
throughout earlier transitions or challenges
in life that required unexpected growth and
stretching. The advice and counsel of a few
others, who insist I should follow in their

footsteps all the way until death, pesters me.
A transition into an individualized life strains
against prescribed expectations, and I could
slowly give up on my expanded growth and
individual desires.

James Hollis writes, "The only antidote
to this form of paralyzing guilt is to step into
choices that enlarge rather than bind us to the
past." This is in part why I find myself stopped
for a season in my progress. The internal messages, well-meant counsel from the past, and
shoulds from concerned family and friends
that arise no longer serve me and must be released, as well as any residual fear and anger.

• • •

What I knew about the elegance of pausing before this process could fit in a thimble.
I've learned that a life filled to the brim and
overflowing with activity (even good works) is
like traveling on the freeway at 80 miles per

hour—no time to savor what's happening, no time to rest. Pausing brings in a motion of a different sort. Stopping for a moment has shown me how my mind races and is unaccustomed to space between thoughts. Initially I hear the call of my youth, "Get back to work this minute!" Then comes the urge to create an exhaustive to-do list. Then my being fills with a sort of nervousness that I'll get behind if I stop. I'm reminded that busyness is a compulsion—an addiction like any other. Another form of clutter that smothers uncomfortable feelings. Not being busy creates a space to face hard questions:

- What if I stop or slow down on a regular basis?
- What if I create some space or downtime between assignments?
- What if I never write again, or want to work again?

• What if I dally? Or moodle? Or nap? Or play?

• What if I want to change my whole life?

• What if I really listen to the yearnings of my heart?

Now, several months away from the winter days I spoke of at the beginning of this chapter, I'm sitting in my backyard garden. It's an overcast day after a week of 100 degree plus weather. Currently there is no wind, so even the leaves of the trees and bushes are motionless. The fronds of the ornamental grass and the long stems above the variegated coral bell leaves are immobile. I wrap myself in green stillness. Below the lists and activities and the restless thinking, the press of doing all the time, is a space for being—full of acceptance, appreciation, compassion, and . . . assurance that I'm on the right path.

I can set a structure and then plan how I

will come in and out of it—when more down time needs to be scheduled, when to get away for a time, when sitting in the garden in the early morning for 45 minutes to practice simply being is the right thing to do. I've set up structure before with my writing. It's time to do it again in a way that lets the rest of my life experience some breathing space, a more restful approach without the pressure of too many things to do. My soul is speaking: "Play with color. Spread out. Be leisurely about it. This will also create an opening for what you want to appear in your writing. Are you getting this? I'm available to help you sort with this kind of dialogue. Give yourself space to rest and incubate and articulate where you are right now. The treasures that will come to light from traveling to the center of your being will become visible."

• • •

The other message surfaces in two
parts—continue to simplify your life even more
in order to create a space for a more meaningful life. Stuff, extra stuff, takes energy to manage. I've made a significant review of what's in
front of me in each room of my home, using
the advice from one author: love it or lose it.
Underneath that I have such an accumulation
of paper, articles, and files filling the corners
and cracks of my home and life. I'm like a
squirrel hoarding food for winter. Now I'm
coming to a deeper level of un-encumbering.
I'm yearning for (and avoiding) the work of
simplifying my life even further. I'm both curious and overwhelmed. Holding on and letting
go—both are complicated. So is the search
for meaning in my life beyond the writing I so
enjoy.

Perhaps new book ideas will keep coming.

I get a feeling that this emergence, this transition into the fullness of myself can take as long as I need to come to a feeling of rightness within. I've had this happen earlier in my life when I felt guided to the right place, the right time, and the right assignment. Doors opened in wondrous ways; new skills and confidence grew exponentially. In contrast, other opportunities I've pursued were experiential, satisfying, and hard work, and required major adjustments because they weren't exactly timed right. Even though I'm struggling now, and have been doing so for some time to feel at peace, I'm at least clear about the process and details. I can take the one next step.

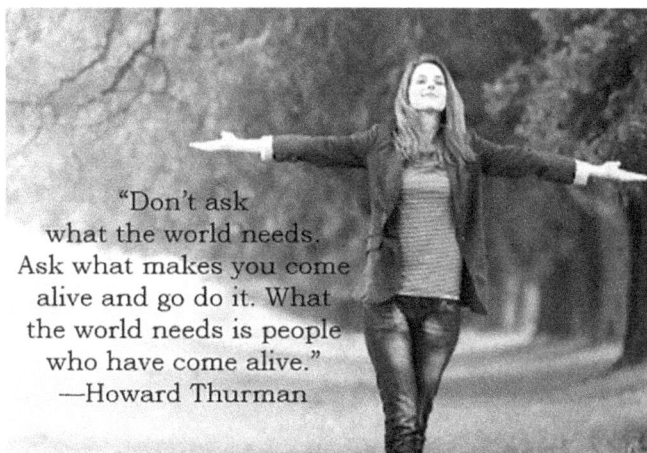

"Don't ask
what the world needs.
Ask what makes you come
alive and go do it. What
the world needs is people
who have come alive."
—Howard Thurman

Chapter 9
Congruence

"Let yourself be silently drawn by the pull of what you really love."
—Rumi

I have come to the end of a decade long inner journey full of twists and turns, resistance, and delays to the beginning of the rest of my life. Some people engage themselves in a similar introspective process in a much shorter time; others breeze through into the wisdom years (60-100) without a pause. I've traveled this journey in the dark. Yet in solitary moments I have felt the presence of unseen angels who have given impressions or suggestions: "go this way, ask this question, read this book, or meet this person."

My circumstances haven't changed as much as I have changed. Life still remains uncertain. How will I finally make peace with this? Effort will not diminish, only the speed is slower and mindfulness and intuition have become more important.

I have gathered into this book a rich saturation of personal introspection, targeted ideas, and concepts that have caused me to rethink my motivations and desires. Another person's call at this stage may be different and individually crafted. For me the message remains constant throughout: "Be still for a season before you move forward." There must be fallow time—a time to gather energy—and incubation time for dreaming and imagining, and then finally development and slower, unhurried steps forward, filled with more quiet space and rest. It's time for the things I want to learn and engage in and time to release disappointments and regrets.

I've learned that like grief, a soul-searching excursion inside, takes as long as it takes for each individual and cannot be rushed. I've asked dozens of questions, many of which I've included in every chapter. As I look back, some answers came early—too early for me to hear. Too much on my plate, too much to do that was engaging or pressing meant no time for solitude, slowing down, or sitting in the sun or shade and enjoying the sweetness of doing nothing.

Some answers distilled slowly like softly falling rain on the dried out and exhausted soil of my soul that hadn't seen nurturing or care in decades. The answers have brought new sets of questions to the surface, as well as clarity about living from a slower-paced place of peace and harmony.

With difficulty I've moved off the hamster wheel and out of the rat race—landing in a frame of mind where I endeavor, for the most part, to preserve mental, emotional, physical, and spiritual health. Now, on some days, I more easily allow stillness to seep into my bones without checking the time or a to-do list. And when my body says, "slow down; create some space around your thinking," I listen. Although changing my thinking about the pacing of my life has been challenging.

Laughingly, my first efforts to slow down included their own to-do lists instead of allowing my intuition to guide me. In an evening moment I practice sitting still and watch the clouds pass through the trees like mystical ghosts—seeping the area with quiet. It's so difficult to calm my fuzzy brain. So I created an acronym for quiet to remind me:

Quit "doing" all the time

Uninterrupted space heals

Introspection opens new pathways

Engage the heart intelligence

Time alone is just fine

The most difficult lesson has been learning
to appreciate life at a much gentler rate and
listen to my body wisdom—the voice that
reminds me that I need regeneration time,
downtime, and solitude built into my enjoyable and busy schedule. Sue Bender says it
best,

> "Learning to listen to my body is like
> having to learn a new language that
> didn't depend on the things I've been
> good at: struggle, effort, and work-
> ing hard all the time. I want to learn
> to move forward with ease; with more
> choices than full speed and collapse."

I need to breathe in and out deeply and slow-

ly, take a break and relax regularly throughout the day. I've found that there's a different
kind of rhythm beyond being driven, when I
cycle between times of exertion and periods of
quiet. It's the pauses that alter the pace.

A part of several transitions I'm expe-
riencing is with my body—healing, releasing
stress, and caring for it in ways I never allowed myself before. I'm working with a massage therapist who also does release work. My
body has been impacted long-term by the fact
that my workaholic tendencies overrule sensi-
ble, balanced living. I have a compulsive habit
of seeing so much to do and accomplishing
much of it without pacing or rest. That leads
to exhaustion and burnout.

I don't know what it would feel like to
be totally rested. I feel like I get within shout-
ing distance sometimes. And yet even when I
can rest, I pop out of bed on the impression

that I have to get started early. I'm not sure
what rest for my soul would be. I wonder if I
could go for a spell without needing something
on my mind—perhaps even go a few days
without reading and just sit and do nothing.
I keep my stack of books high. I don't know
about rest from gardening or cooking. How did
I get to my 60's and not have that somewhat
figured out? I want white space and time to
study Spanish. I'm so weary, that desire has
slid off my plate. The exhaustion I feel regularly—where I put one foot in front of the other
and move, may have to do with being in transition. This takes time and energy and unencumbering from anything, like clutter. I want
time to putter or sort through stuff without a
deadline, or read leisurely, or choose not go to
some family event.

William Bridges states: "It isn't the
changes that do us in, it's the transitions.

Change is not the same as transition. Change is external; transition is internal. There can be any number of changes, but unless there are transitions, nothing will be different when the dust settles."

Physical exercise and stretching are now priorities and consistent. Mind work is improving. Listening to my body has given me a list, like a prescription:

• Set more closed boundaries. When concerns arise, release these. Internalizing worries—personalizing them—hits the adrenal glands and makes it difficult to maintain hormonal balance. As Elizabeth Gilbert suggests, "Send love and light," so I release those concerns on the sunshine.

• Develop a slower rhythm. Schedule time away once a quarter. Pause often during the day. Plan an afternoon once or twice a week for play. Pay attention to breathing.

Tenseness leads to shallow breathing. Relax; move through projects and plans unhurried.

• Drink plenty of water; dehydration leads to confusion. Eat smaller nutritious meals a day. Eliminate sugar.

All of these messages have come in still moments. If my body could talk, it would say, "I'm worn down. Slow down, rest, and stop being frantic." My lymph system says, "I'm working slowly, sluggishly. Labeling life as uncertain has created hidden pockets of stress. Now do more relaxation, deep breathing, and meditation. Focus in your heart area and breathe into your heart. Your shallow breathing began between ages 8-13 when you closed down expression of self-knowledge." (Wow!) These days I'm releasing any residual childhood hurts, adult disappointments, allowing forgiveness of others and myself to soak into my cells.

This has to do with establishing clear

boundaries and letting go of the pressured expectation that I'm supposed to be on call most of the time. During a guided imagery, I imagined a semi-permeable boundary between others and myself. I held the symbol of a chain-link fence in my left hand that I felt needed to be established as a brick wall in my right hand. This was because it brought back an unexpected feeling from childhood—learning to be helpful every hour of every day. I've transferred that expectation to my current family, so it's recent, and also the old patterns and some resentment contributing to the tired feelings.

Christiane Northup explains, "During our fifties we may come up against the unfinished business that we have accumulated over the first half of life—as if we've gone into the basement and found boxes of stuff to be sorted through and weeded out. Fatigue is a message from our inner guidance that a repressed or forgotten part of our life needs attention."

The surprising and transforming boundary I held in my right hand is not rigid at all. Instead of a brick wall, it's a rosy light radiating from my heart; a light that honors my need for space, free from that feeling that I need to be available for others at any time. I'm at liberty to bracket time for my own thriving and growth, *and* stay connected with the family relationships I love and cherish without compromising my health. I include myself within the family circle of desires instead of leaving what I want to the last after everyone else's, or not at all.

When I'm more balanced, I've also unhooked from worrying all the time. In the past I've masked worry to those around me in a way that embedded it into every part of my being. I could appear calm and at ease on the outside, and be tied up in knots inside; tense, stiff, and afraid. Worry means I have the best answers for someone else's life. Now I don't have to have all the answers for anyone. I can be curious and patient instead. When I feel anger, fear, hopelessness, or disappointment, I can give unconditional love from my heart.

I've used busyness to avoid anxiety in the face of uncertainty. Slowing down has forced me to face my dis-ease with stillness, release unproductive worry and anxiety, and reframe several limiting assumptions. I've learned that avoiding risk won't keep me safe, and that risk includes stumbling blocks, obstacles, setbacks, even helpful delays that set me up for ultimately life-enhancing lessons. Grumbling doesn't help; resiliency—the ability to rebound in the face of trials and see the possibilities—does. Greg LeVoy suggests that we ask our setbacks, "What are you trying to

teach me?" "Where is my life attempting to
go?" The challenges teach me humility and reveal my ability to prevail with grace and gratitude in the face of struggles.

I'm coming to a place of peace in the
journey of the inner transition I've been in for
the past several years: at ease with not knowing. I'm examining everything and want to quit
what doesn't work. The best question I ask is,
"Am I using complaining as a problem-solving
technique? If I'm complaining, then either let
go or take action. What's the best use of my
time right now?

I've found my way to the center of my
being—to the creative part of myself—the
part that enjoys peaceful instrumental music,
painting, writing, piecing a quilt, gardening,
and contemplation. These feed the child in me
that has always hungered for creative outlets.

My days are as cluttered as my office

most of the time. Even without a to-do list I look around and feel swamped. Unencumbering is a constant chore. I'm looking for that deep place of peace and flow. Not the kind of flow that is productivity and getting lots done. When I'm in flow I'm not in linear time, I'm in the moment. I want more of that. The best change in perception is to not label myself inefficient and beat myself up when I only get one thing done in a day instead of ten. I'm feeling my way forward, and, as Dave Whyte states, "using my intuition to live within the boundary between chaos and order where rest and action move together" without pushing all the time. I remember that when I'm impatient, it clouds my perspective. I forget to love the process of growth I have chosen.

Seeking the best energy for healing and well-being is not selfish. What energy do I need to release in order to allow what nourishes me to come in? SARK says, "Healing happens in spirals and layers and inside interior crevices." I have felt healing happen this way. Life provides me with a panorama of experiences that allow me to keep running into myself. I continually practice releasing all negative feelings, blame, and control. Everything in my life is an opportunity to grow. I'm grateful for the lessons. The transformation comes as I live so that my inner life shows more clearly on the outside.

This is the time for deep listening. Every day is a balancing act as I learn to listen for what I'm feeling drawn to. I still practice stillness. Already in my life, from time to time, God has whispered into my heart, confirming my belief that a certain pathway has His approval and delight. I can wait patiently for that confirmation. I've learned that there will be a sign when the time is right to take flight again like the butterfly that has dried its wings and is ready. Then I will start moving gently forward in the sunlight.

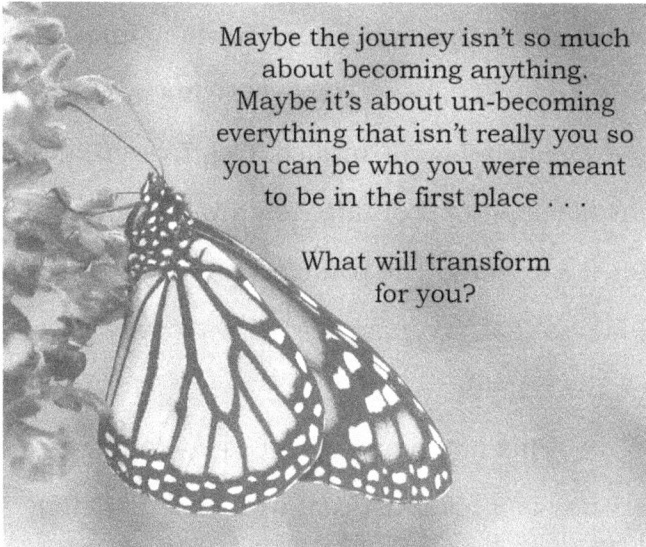

Maybe the journey isn't so much about becoming anything. Maybe it's about un-becoming everything that isn't really you so you can be who you were meant to be in the first place . . .

What will transform for you?

Resources

Arrien, Angeles, (2007) *The Second Half of Life*, Boulder, Co: Sounds True.

Austin, Linda, (2000) *What's Holding You Back?* New York, NY: Basic Books.

Bender, Sue, (1995) *Everyday Sacred*, New York, NY: HarperCollins.

Bode, Richard, (1993) *First You Have to Row a Little Boat*, New York, NY: Warner Books.

Brehony, Kathleen A., (1996) *Awakening at Midlife*, New York, NY: Riverhead Books.

Bridges, William, (2004) *Transitions*, Cambridge Massachusetts: Da Capo Press.

Briggs, John, and Peat, F. David, (1999) *Seven Life Lessons of Chaos*, New York, NY: Harper-Collins.

Brown, Brene, (2010) *The Gifts of Imperfection*, Center City, Minneota: Hazelden.

Campbell, Joseph, (2008) *The Hero with a Thousand Faces*, Novato, CA: New World Library.

Childre, Doc and Martin, Howard, (1999) *The HeartMath Solution*, New York, NY: HarperCollins.

Coelho, Paulo, (1994) *The Alchemist*, San Francisco, CA: HarperCollins.

Estes, Clarissa Pinkola, (1992) *Women Who Run With The Wolves*, New York, NY; Ballantyne Books.

Gilbert, Elizabeth, (2006) *Eat, Pray, Love*, New York, NY: Penguin Group.

Hendrix, Harville, *Oprah Magazine*, January 2001, p. 56, "Reconnecting."

Hollis, James, (2005) *Finding Meaning in the Second Half of Life*, New York, NY: Gotham Books.

Kidd, Sue Monk, ((1990) *When the Heart Waits*, New York, NY: HarperOne.

L'Engle, Madeleine, (1972) *The Circle of Quiet*, San Francisco: Harper & Row Publishers.

LeVoy, Greg, (1997) *Callings*, New York, NY: Three Rivers Press.

London, Peter, (1989) *No More Secondhand Art*, Boston, Massachusetts: Shambhala Publications, Inc.

Markova, Dawna, (2000) *I Will Not Die an Unlived Life*, Boston, MA: Conari Press.

Murdock, Maureen, (1990) *The Heroine's Journey*, Boston, Massachusetts: Shambhala Publications, Inc.

SARK, (2008) *Juicy Pens Thirsty Paper*, New York, NY: Three Rivers Press.

Sheehy, Gail, (1976) *Passages*, New York, NY: Bantam Books, Inc.

Sinetar, Marsha, (1998) *The Mentor's Spirit*, New York, NY: St. Martin's Griffin.

Tolle, Eckhart, (2005) *A New Earth*, New YorkNY: Dutton.

Tsabary, Stefali, (2010) *The Conscious Parent*, Vancouver, Canada: Namaste Publishing.

Ueland, Brenda, (1987) *If You Want to Write*, St. Paul, Minnesota: Graywolf Press.

Ulrich, Wendy, (2012) *The Temple Experience*, Springville, UT: Cedar Fort, Inc.

Whyte, Dave, (1994) *The Heart Aroused*, New York, NY: Doubleday.

Acknowledgements

I've been a student of life's transitions. The latest shift into midlife surprised me more than I expected because it seemed to require more of a step inward rather than forward. As I studied what others had written, I felt impressed to document my own journey.

Many thanks to my writers' group: Linda O., Norma, Betty, Phyllis, Sherri, Rene, Estell, and Linda C. who listened and gave dozens of helpful suggestions and edits on each chapter as it emerged and then re-emerged years later in a totally different form.

I've also had tremendous support from my assistant, Julie Hill, as well as other friends and relatives who were readers for me, and engaged in numerous conversations about this interior journey.

I'm deeply grateful to my family, especially my husband Stan, for supporting my curiosity and my love of writing.

www.ingramcontent.com/pod-product-compliance
Lightning Source LLC
Chambersburg PA
CBHW031548040426
42452CB00006B/237